THE COMPLETE MAN

Achieve Ultimate Performance, Fulfillment and Victory in EVERY Area of Your Life

PURDEEP SANGHA, EMBA

THE COMPLETE MAN

Achieve Ultimate Performance, Fulfillment and Victory in EVERY Area of Your Life

Paperback ISBN: 978-1-7353738-2-9
Hardcover ISBN: 978-1-7353738-3-6

Design by Transcendent Publishing
Edited by Mitch Sisskind

The author of this book does not dispense medical advice or prescribe the use of any technique as a form of treatment for mental, physical, emotional, or medical problems without the advice of a physician, either directly or indirectly. The intent of the author is only to offer information of a general nature to help you in your quest for mental, emotional, physical, and spiritual well-being. In the event you use any of the information in this book for yourself, the author and the publisher assume no responsibility for your actions. The author makes no guarantees concerning the level of success you may experience by following the advice and strategies contained in this book.

Printed in the Unites States of America.

DEDICATION

This book is dedicated to hard-working husbands, fathers, and all men who strive to provide the best lives possible for their families. In loving memory of my father, Lakhbir Sangha (1954 – 2018).

CONTENTS

INTRODUCTION

As my wife walked into the family room, tears were pouring down her face.

She tried to speak. "It's dad…he's gone."

Needless to say, this was a shock. My father was gone and would never return. My first thought was about my mom. Was she okay? She never dealt well with death at all. When she heard of a loved one's passing, she would go into a genuine panic.

So many questions were flooding my brain. What led to my father's passing? Did he pass peacefully? Or did he suffer? And why now? My parents lived in British Columbia, and we were near Toronto. Why couldn't he wait until I could see him one more time?

But all those questions were irrelevant now, weren't they? He was gone. Nothing was going to change it.

I phoned my aunt, who was with my mother. She described how my dad and my mom had gotten into a little argument the night before he died. That wasn't exactly a surprise. They had been married for forty years and I'd seen them argue many times. Often, it was due to my dad drinking a little more than he should have.

In any case, mom got up the next morning as usual. It was Sunday, and she decided to go to the Sikh temple for prayer. She typically drags my dad along with her, but because she was upset with him, she went on her own. Before she left, she did make his lunch for him. She knew my dad had a big appetite and she always made sure he had good meals.

While my mom was at the temple, my dad went out to work in the orchard as he usually did when he was bored. When my mom came home, she noticed that he had not eaten his lunch. That wasn't like him. But she could hear the "chipmunk" running so she didn't think anything of it.

The chipmunk is similar to a construction lift, but more fun. It has three wheels. You stand on a platform and maneuver your way through the orchard at various heights to cut the top branches of the trees. It was my dad's favorite piece of equipment.

Because my mom thought my dad was just working, she went out into the orchard and started working herself. That was my mom, a working woman that worked just as hard, if not harder than my dad.

After an hour or so, my mom began to worry. It was unusual for dad not to eat, which could be dangerous because of his diabetes. She decided to look for him, and found him lying on the ground, completely still, with his arms at his sides. He hadn't fallen. It was as if he'd just fallen asleep.

A worker in the neighboring orchard heard her scream and hurried over. Later, he said it sounded like an animal was caught in a trap. By the time an ambulance came, it was too late.

My mom replays that day over and over again. She has so many "what ifs." What if they had not quarreled the night before? What if she had said "hi" to him in the morning? What if she had taken him to the temple? He may not have suffered when he passed, but she is in pain as she lives.

My dad was a hard-working man who came to Canada from India in the 1970's with only $11. He and my mom had little education and could barely speak English, but they knew how to work hard. They worked for years in orchards for close to the minimum wage, and finally they were able to buy an orchard of their own.

They created a good life in Canada. Because he had his own business, my father eventually had the freedom to spend his days as he wanted. But from as far back as I can remember, I sensed that something was missing for him. He and my mom had a good relationship, but it wasn't passionate. My dad had friends but no one he could really open up with. He did drink, which worsened the diabetes which led to his fatal heart attack.

My dad envisioned the age of 65 as an important milestone. He told himself that at 65 he would have really "done it." He came from India with next to nothing and created a life for himself and his family. He was going to pull back from work and travel more. We were planning a vacation with my brother and his wife, and every year after that we would all travel together to new places. His moment to be proud was going to be 65, but he died at the age of 64 and a half.

What About You?

On the surface everything may look great, but inside you're feeling incomplete. You hope for more, and you believe that what you're looking for will happen with time, but so far it hasn't happened. You're in one of the three situations that, based on my experience, the vast majority of men inhabit.

- You envision a lifestyle for yourself and your family but it seems like it's taking you forever to achieve it. Life feels like it's passing you by.
- You're experiencing a level of success in one area of your life, like your business or career, but you're having difficulty balancing that with your relationships, family, and personal enjoyment. Living one dimensionally is costing you.
- You've got everything you want but you're still not feeling the joy and fulfillment you want. You've almost lost your passion for life.

In all three of these situations, you may feel like your life is a life that others want you to live, not the life you really want.

I almost fell into that trap. I was living in the corporate rat race as a "successful" executive, making great money with all the status and the perks. But I was also in a failing relationship with my wife and was unfulfilled with my life overall. I was going through the motions without feeling fully alive and passionate. I was living a version of my dad's life in a different context.

My dad's passing was a sign for me. He seemed to be telling me something very specific and very powerful: "Son, there are men out there who need your help."

When I thought about this, I realized that I had always been interested in helping people improve their lives. From an early age, I studied how men behaved because I wanted to help my dad overcome his alcohol addiction. I was the only one in our household who could calm him down when he drank too much. I knew his behavior better than he did. I knew when he was going to drink before he even knew it.

Over the years I watched men and studied how they operated. I observed the dynamics of relationships between men and women, and between men and society as a whole. I started to recognize patterns in men who were complete, and in those who were not.

I went on to develop my skills in business school and in my career. I specialized in studies of neuroscience, psychology, and spirituality. I spent 14 years in the corporate world, and started my consulting and coaching firm for entrepreneurs and executives. I went from wanting to be a CEO of a major corporation to coaching some of the top CEOs around the world.

At first, I focused on helping men improve their business acumen. But this soon became more about them as men and less about their business. As I started to develop a reputation, even women began referring their male business partners or husbands to me.

Then my dad died, and I heard what he seemed to be telling me. I made the decision to go all in on working with men to help them get what they want from their work and their lives. To help them have it all. To help them become complete.

Now I live life on my terms. I'm helping men feel complete and fulfilled regardless of what comes their way, and that's how I feel too.

Can you have everything you want? That is, everything you really want, not what you're supposed to want or what someone tells you to want?

The answer is "yes." Too many men are faking it, but you'll truly have it.

Men are multi-faceted beings. You are not as simple as society makes you out to be. Becoming The Complete Man can't be Googled. It's not something you can experience just by taking a course, attending a seminar, or listening to a motivational speaker. Unfortunately, many of those speakers are incomplete themselves. They may help you in one area of life, but not all. That's why this book addresses all aspects of a man's life, from career to relationships to fatherhood. We've all heard about bucket lists. Your life includes many different buckets and all of them deserve to be filled. Those who focus on just one bucket are making a mistake. Those who fill all the buckets are complete men. They have it all!

Becoming "The Complete Man"

Developing yourself as a Complete Man comes from making a series of decisions and actions that empower you to create the life you want. It's like playing chess but with much more at stake. Every move in a chess game has consequences, but unless you're a skilled player, you're likely oblivious of the results your moves will have. That's exactly how an inComplete Man goes through life.

Without even realizing it, you could be making key decisions based on habit rather than a full awareness of what you really want. If your habit-based decisions are taking you in the wrong direction, you need to change your habits, or your decision-making process, or both. But first, you need to be aware of them.

The chapters in this book will enable you to identify behaviors, patterns, internal mindsets, and emotions that are holding you back. You'll discover what you need to adjust in yourself, in your life, and you'll also learn how to do it with the least amount of time and effort.

Toward that goal, here's a first all-important point. To have a complete life, you must first be complete in your inner world. An inComplete Man on the inside will have an incomplete life on the outside. Your external world is a reflection and an expression of what's inside you.

Manipulating your external environment in order to change your internal world is futile. You'll most likely waste a lot of time, effort, resources, and energy with few positive results to show for it. If you have inner abundance and fulfillment, you will experience that in your life as a whole. If you have emptiness and stress inside of you, you'll find that on the outside as well.

In short, *being* is far more important than *having*. Even a rich man will feel poor if he's not already rich on the inside. But if your inner world is abundant, your external world will be as well.

Thought vs Feeling

Every decision you make and every action you take is based on a feeling, not a thought. You may have a specific thought in mind, but that thought derives from an underlying feeling. You want to achieve success, for example, because it will make you feel a certain way. You want to have a better relationship because of the emotions that you will enjoy. Whether you know it or not, everything you want is associated with a feeling.

Every decision you've made during your lifetime has led you to who you are and what you have or don't have right now. When you come to understand the emotional foundations of your decisions and act accordingly, your external world will immediately respond.

The effect will be like opening the gates of a dam and letting the water flow. Your wants will start flowing to you effortlessly. What seemed impossible before will become possible. What was causing you pain and anxiety will no longer bother you. What seemed difficult will become easy. What you were chasing will be drawn to you like a magnet.

The Three Frameworks of Inner Power

There are powerful forces within you that, once unlocked, will cause everyone and everything around you to respond. That's the everyday experience of The Complete Man. But an inComplete Man is living to only a fraction of his capabilities, and the power inside him lies dormant.

By learning to unlock the power within you, you will no longer feel that your life is like pounding on a brick wall that never moves at all. Your life will flow in the direction you want. Even if you do come up against some resistance, it will inevitably crumble at your feet.

As a first step toward making this happen, I've defined three frameworks for understanding and organizing your life.

- **The Achievement Framework** through which you can achieve your goals faster and easier.

- **The Performance Framework**, a system for consistently performing at your highest potential.
- **The Fulfillment Framework**, including the strategies to master the thoughts, feelings, and energy you need to live a truly passionate, joyful and complete life.

To understand the frameworks, imagine yourself driving in a Formula 1 car race. You will need all three systems to win the race.

The Achievement Framework is your engine. It's the physical manifestation of your inner power.

The Performance Framework is your car's transmission. It's the bridge between your engine's power and the results that happen when that power is applied in the real world.

Then there's Fulfillment Framework. Whatever the tangible achievements of your life may be, the real reward is the feeling of completion that you achieve. Remember: every thought and every action begins with a feeling and reaches completion with a feeling. Everything begins with a feeling of desire, and can end with a feeling of fulfillment. Whether it does end in fulfillment is entirely up to you. The more in tune you are with the three frameworks, the better your chances for completion.

The Thirteen C's of the Complete Package

Within each of the Three Frameworks are thirteen specific elements whose presence will make the difference between completion and anything less. The greater the presence of these elements, the closer you will come to fulfillment as a Complete Man.

1. **Cause** – What is your motivation for getting out of bed each day and living each moment at the highest level of your being?

2. **Clarity** – This is a precise and complete understanding of your life's direction.

3. **Confidence** – An unshakeable belief in your ability to meet your responsibilities and achieve your goals.

4. **Courage** – Strength to confront your fears without hesitation and to take action in overcoming them.

5. **Certainty** – Complete faith that you can and will "have it all." The phrase "maybe in my next life" never enters your mind!

6. **Control** – You are the master of your inner being regardless of any and all external circumstances.

7. **Commitment** – Unwavering dedication to becoming a Complete Man.

8. **Consistency** – Achieving results at the highest level each and every time.

9. **Capacity** – You make the space and have the energy to take on whatever needs to be done without reducing the quality of your life.

10. **Creativity** – The ability to discover solutions to your challenges that are desirable, practical, and fulfilling.

11. **Competitiveness** – Not competition with others, but yearning desire to evolve and grow.

12. **Contentment** – Being peaceful and happy with yourself and your life regardless of external circumstances.

13. **Character** – Thinking, acting, feeling, and living as a Complete Man.

The Biggest Mistakes That Men Make

There's a saying that you can't always make a situation better, but you can always make it worse. I would add that you can make a situation worse without even realizing it, and that's a big mistake.

In my opinion, based on years of working with hundreds of men, let's look at the biggest mistakes you can make:

- **The Lone Ranger approach** – You don't admit to yourself and others that you can use some help. You would rather struggle on your own because you think that's what men are supposed to do.
- **Suffering is a part of success** – You believe that you must suffer in some way to achieve the life you want, as if suffering were a rite of passage.
- **Settling** – You resign yourself to having less than the best in some area of your life. You don't believe you can have it all, or you don't believe that you deserve it.
- **Attaining vs being** – You focus on attaining goals, titles, money and other externals rather than being The Complete Man.
- **One dimensional living** – You become preoccupied with specific areas of your life while ignoring others.
- **Working harder to attain more** – You believe that simply working harder and longer gets you what you want.
- **Spinning your wheels** – When things aren't working out for you, you keep trying one new thing after the other without getting any traction.
- **Focus on the external** – You fail to realize that everything you desire in your material environment will only come to you when you change your internal being.
- **Wait and hope** – You hope that you will reach the day when you'll have and experience what you want, rather than making that day come to you.
- **Burnout** – You work your butt off without enjoying your life. You may even be putting yourself at risk of serious health issues.

- **Inauthentic self** – You become a man that others want you to be and live a life that others want you to live.

We all make mistakes, but I believe that learning from our mistakes is highly overrated. It's much easier to avoid mistakes in the first place. So, please think about this list carefully. Do you recognize yourself in any of the categories, or perhaps in more than one of them? Or can you think of mistakes you're making that aren't on the list? If not, great! If so, now is a good time to change.

PART ONE

The Achievement Framework

Right now, you may have an important goal in mind, but your progress towards it is slower than you expected, or you may not be making any progress at all, or you might even be going backwards. You're watching other men around you experience success, and you're wondering what you're doing wrong.

The Achievement Framework offers a system for reaching your goals quickly and with less stress...

> **The Achievement Framework =**
> **Premium Goals + Identity + Systems**

CHAPTER ONE

What Men Want

"Freedom is the ability to do what you want, when you want, and to live the life you want."

-Purdeep Sangha

I planned on being the CEO of a major corporation and I was well on my way to achieving it. I had a gorgeous wife and two gorgeous kids. I had the perks of being an executive and the status that came with it.

But something inside me still wasn't fulfilled. I felt like someone else was in control of my life. I was pleasing others more than I was pleasing myself. Getting up, going to work and doing the same things over and over. As long as I stayed on this path, my parents were happy, my wife was happy, my kids were happy, but I wasn't happy. I wasn't Complete.

One Sunday I sat down and read a series of passages from books by spiritual leaders and philosophers. Something came over me that day. It was a moment of clarity. I told myself that I was going to take control of my life and live it on my terms.

I walked into work a couple of days later and quit. My manager asked if I really wanted to do this and I answered, "Yes, it's time that I move on." I walked out of that building with my belongings that same day.

My colleagues were shocked. Some thought that I was fired.

A few thought that I had an accident and hurt my head. Amusing theories, but none were correct. I was going to create the life I wanted to live.

It wasn't easy. I had been groomed to think, act, behave, write and even speak a certain way as an executive. I almost forgot who I was. It took me almost a year to reshape my identity.

I had to set boundaries with my parents and my wife. They had thought that I had thrown everything away, that over a decade of climbing the corporate ladder had gone to waste. But I would ignore them if they spoke negatively about my new path.

My wife was generally supportive but there were times when she was scared. I couldn't give up. This was my one shot to do what I believed I was meant to do. Those challenges were worthwhile, because I learned so much about myself and how to live on my own terms.

Now, I get up every morning doing what I want to do and living how I want to live. I love it!

What Men Really Want

Ask a man what he really wants, and he will tell you what he thinks is appropriate or what he's been conditioned to believe. But deep down men have two burning desires. The first is to feel complete inside. The second is to experience victory and have it all in life. Not aspiring to have it all isn't being humble, it's being foolish. You were meant to have it all. That's why you were put on this Earth.

But let's be clear about what victory means to a Complete Man. It doesn't mean scoring more points than the other guy or reaching the finish line first. Victory means getting past the internal barriers, most of which are self-created, that restrict your freedom to become the man you have the potential to be.

That's the victory you really want and deserve. Men crave the freedom to be The Complete Man. No man wakes up in the morning thinking, "I feel like being miserable today. I'm going to be someone else's bitch." But many men go through their entire lives living that way, following a path someone else has designed. Screw that!

Be the man you'll feel proud of being. If you want to be a full-time dad, be a full-time dad. If you want to be the governor of the state, be the governor of the state. But don't be what others are telling you to be. I don't recommend that you walk into work and quit tomorrow. But I do recommend that you sit down and determine whether you're living life the way you want to live it.

Passionate Relationship

You want to be in a passionate relationship with lots of sex, right? You want to be desired by your woman or by numerous women. If you don't have a passionate relationship, you truly are missing out. It's one of the most fulfilling aspects of life.

People who tell you that it's not possible to have an amazing relationship are just naysayers who are looking to justify their own failures. My grandparents were married for 60 years before they both passed away. When my grandfather died, my grandmother was deeply saddened by the loss of her partner in life. She passed away a year after my grandfather did. I could tell that they truly loved and respected each other. They spent an entire lifetime cherishing one another. It definitely can be done.

Wealth

Wealth comes in many different forms. For example, you may be a father who decides to spend more time with your children than building your career. Your wealth takes the form of watching your kids grow up to be wonderful people.

But for the moment, let's think of wealth as money. Money is a byproduct of providing value to others that they are willing to pay for. I've worked with very successful men who have all the monetary wealth you can dream of. Most of them will tell you that their money doesn't really make them happy. Yes, money allows you to pay your bills, to provide for your family, and to avoid problems that a large proportion of the world's population struggles with. But as the saying goes, money isn't everything. My friend's neighbor is an extremely wealthy man and both of his sons died of unnatural causes. It's rumored that they committed suicide because they didn't get the guidance they needed from their father, who was preoccupied with building his business. My friend tells me that his neighbor is looking at life a lot differently now.

Money is great to have and you deserve to have a ton of it. My parents used to say, "Money doesn't grow on trees." I would tell them to look outside at the orchard, because, for us, money did grow on trees. Then my parents would give me that stern look like I was going to get a whack across the head.

I grew up with the belief that too much money corrupts people. No wonder my bank account was empty for most of my life until I realized that I had to look at money from a new perspective. I decided to see money as an avenue to do more good things for people and animals.

When my kids are a little older, my goal is to take my family around the world and build animal shelters and educate the population about the importance of treating animals and the earth with respect. It's a heck of a lot easier to do this with money than not having money. What do you want to do with your wealth?

Time

If you don't have the time to spend with your family and time for the things you enjoy, what's the point? You have a finite amount of time in your life. Life has the same ending for every person on this planet, and we never know when the end will come. So, use your time doing what you enjoy.

I spent years eating breakfast and lunch at my desk. I rushed through my workouts so I could get back to work. I love food and I love working out but I was rushing through everything to sit at my desk and look at a computer screen. Now I eat at the dinner table and take my time during my workouts. I'm even more productive because I allow myself downtime.

Do you feel like you wake up on Monday, go to sleep, and then wake up to Monday again? I felt this way for years. It's important to look at time as moments rather than hours and minutes. By doing this, you don't need to rush. If you want the moment to last longer, you can indulge in it. You can't create more time, but you can create more pleasurable time for yourself.

Here's a simple exercise to help with this. Take a sheet of paper, draw a line down the middle, write the heading "Must Do" on one side and "Like To Do" on the other. Write down everything you do in a day in the appropriate columns. Then challenge yourself to remove the Must Do's from your life by delegating, hiring someone or removing them all together.

Watch out for your own excuses. You may end up telling yourself that you can't afford to delegate it or someone else can't do it as well as you or other excuses. Be creative in determining how to outsource the Must Do's so you have more time to do what you like. Of course, there will always be some Must Do's that you need to keep. If you don't like exercise, for instance, you can't get someone else to exercise for you.

Options

The Complete Men I know have options to fully experience life.

They can start a new business, or they can take vacations for months because their business operates itself. Having options isn't just about having the money. I know men who have very little money but they are connected with the coolest people and have the ability to travel wherever they want.

If you don't have options, you feel trapped. When my relationship was at a low point, I felt like I had no options and having no options felt worse than the relationship itself. Now it's my choice to be in my marriage. This empowers me to be a better husband, and also ask my wife for what I need.

Whenever you feel stuck, it's because you're stuck in your thinking. One of the first things to do is create a list of options. The more options you create, the more choices you have and the greater your chances of getting what you want. You'll be surprised by how many options you actually have.

Status

Maybe it's at work, maybe it's at the gym, or maybe it's at a party where there are attractive women around, but you're always evaluating your status compared to others.

That's normal. The human brain has a natural tendency to focus on hierarchy. Society paints a picture that the more status you have, the more wealth you have, the more freedom you have, the more respect you have, the more sex you have and the more love you have.

Avoiding status would be unnatural because you are literally hardwired for it. The moment you enter a room with other men, you are determining where you are superior and inferior to others without even knowing it. The moment you rank higher than another man, you have greater confidence, the moment you rank lower, your confidence drops. If you rank lower than a woman, your confidence drops even lower. It's an unconscious reaction but you can learn to take conscious control.

Status can be a puppeteer. There's no shortage of men who base their worth on their job title or net worth, only to have the rug pulled from under them when they lose their jobs or wealth. Appreciate status but don't be controlled by it. I teach men to create status based on their own terms. When you rank yourself on your own scale, you have the internal competitiveness of The Complete Man. When you compare your current self to your former self from a year ago, you can't help but feel great.

Respect and Admiration

Men want to be respected for who they are. Having respect means that your sacrifices, long hours, commitment to your goals, and efforts are appreciated. You especially want to be respected by your wife and kids because you would do anything for them.

You work hard to give your family the life they deserve or you go out of your way to help others in need. You don't seek praise but respect at a minimum. But if you spend your entire life sacrificing and providing for your wife and kids with little respect in return, this will eventually lead to resentment, avoidance, or even victim mentality. If you're not respected for what you do, dig deep and find out why. A man shouldn't demand respect, but respect should be given where deserved.

To Be Loved

Love is such an amazing feeling but you don't hear a lot of men talking about love. The truth is that you want to be loved and loved all the time. You want to be loved by your parents, by your wife, your kids, your employees, your neighbors and your dog. The more love you get, the more alive you feel.

I have to put my ego aside some days and tell my wife, "I

need you to love me today." I'm not ashamed of it and I don't feel any less of a man. I feel more like a man because I get that love that I ask for. When you want more fulfillment in your life, the easiest way to get it is with love.

You cannot give or receive enough love. It is the most powerful feeling and it enables you to do powerful things. Love can cure many conditions such as issues with health, broken relationships and even broken spirits. I believe that love is the most natural and powerful force in this universe.

Progress

If I told you that you would be in the exact same position one year from now, how would you feel? You wouldn't be happy, I'm sure. What if I told you that you would make less than half the money you did this year? You would probably freak out. Progress is like fuel. A little bit can keep you going and a lot can light you up like a firecracker.

If you are always growing as an individual by learning new skills, deepening your relationships, or learning more about yourself, you will be more fulfilled than those who are not growing. Progress doesn't have to be external to feel valuable. You can grow your wealth by 10 times and still feel like you're stuck in the same place. Or you can learn a new skill and feel on top of the world. And your internal progress will eventually lead to external progress as well.

For years, I felt subpar compared to many of my schoolmates and friends. Some of them went on to amass great wealth soon after university and others became professionals like doctors or lawyers.

I was learning about human potential and what makes people perform and be fulfilled. I was obsessed with mastering myself. It finally hit me that I had two decades of internal progress that most of my friends and schoolmates didn't have. It was much easier to obtain the external things from years of internal progress. It's much harder for them to obtain the internal things even though they have the externals already. Your internal progress is your secret weapon.

Vitality

Men need health and energy to enjoy life to the fullest. You don't want to spend your entire day at work only to come home exhausted. It leaves you with little energy for your wife and kids and the things you enjoy doing. You want to have the vitality to experience life with a full battery, not a battery that constantly needs to be recharged.

If vitality isn't high on your list, it will be at some point. There's a tipping point, typically later in a man's life, when he realizes that his vitality is the most important priority. Having everything in life only makes sense if you have the vitality to fully enjoy it.

Control

Men want control, but the only thing you can really control is yourself. The more you let go of trying to control your external world, the more you are genuinely in control. You can't control how your wife acts or how your children act or how your in-laws act. You can only influence the people around you; you cannot control them. But you do have total control over your inner world which includes your thoughts, your emotions, and your energy.

Control over your external world is a perception. If you've lost someone very close to you, you know that you had no control over that. Their time had come and there wasn't much you could do about it. The one thing you can control is how you react to situations. The more control you have over yourself, the better your quality of life will be.

Summary Action Items

1. Write down what you want in life.

2. Go for having it all and not settling.

3. Be aware of the illusive traps like status that may throw you off track.

CHAPTER TWO

....

Premium Goals

"The moment you put a deadline on your dream it becomes a goal."

-Stephen Kellogg

Randy came to me asking to be coached. He had a successful business that he wanted to expand and capture additional opportunities in his market. His business was growing at a rate of five percent annually but he thought that was low compared to what was possible. We discussed his business for about an hour over a Zoom call and I asked him specific questions.

"How much do you want to increase your revenues?"

"I'd like to double my annual revenues."

"What do you want to do with those revenues?"

"I want to pay off some debt...."

At the end of the conversation, I said, "Randy, when you wake up in the morning, do your goals get you fired up?"

He looked away from the screen and said, "I guess they do."

But that was not the right answer. Like most men, Randy was without what I call premium goals. I could see why he was only growing his business at five percent each year. His goals were average at best.

If you have average quality, you won't be inspired, motivated, and committed to achieving your goals.

How often have you set a goal and dropped it months later? Or you set a goal and didn't take any action at all? Experts say that goal-setting increases chances of success, but this is not entirely true. You need premium goals to increase your chances.

What is a Premium Goal?

In any situation, if you had the choice between average, good or premium, which would you choose? I assume you would choose premium. Why wouldn't you choose the best? The same applies to your goals.

Premium goals are the ones that get you fired up and draw you towards them rather than you having to constantly push yourself. It's the difference between tirelessly pushing a snowball up a hill or watching it roll down the other side under its own force. A goal should challenge you and challenge you to grow, but it shouldn't feel like just another obligation. That's a chore, not a goal.

Amazingly, goal-setting isn't really taught and it's a shame. People just tell you to write them down and look at them every day but there are other components to premium goals that increase your chances of achieving them.

Your Vision

Goals should be more than a list of words on paper. They should be part of who you are. So, before you do any goal-setting, you should have a vision for your life.

To get started with this, pick a time in the future and describe your ideal life. If nothing stood in your way, what would your life look like? Take a few minutes to do this right now.

This isn't as easy as it sounds. You probably tell yourself, "That's not possible. I'd have to win the lottery." But I want you to remove every negative thought in your mind. Think big. Think really big. What do you want your life to be like? The universe has a way of responding to those who ask.

This vision itself isn't your goal. Your vision is how your life is going to turn out in the future. Goals are meant to be more specific. Your vision is like the north star, directing your overall path. Your vision should be flexible because life changes over time and so will your vision. Your vision 20 years ago probably wasn't the same one you have now.

3-3-3

Can you have too many goals? In my opinion, you can. If you're the type of person who has goals for everything, you might be spreading yourself thin. Keeping goals simple and easy is the best way to stay on track and not forget them.

In the past, I had goals for almost everything in life, from my weight to how many calories I would digest to the amount of cardio I would do each day. I couldn't even keep track of all my goals. The fact is, your brain is geared to think in chunks of three's. Anything greater is harder for your mind to track.

Most men have three main buckets in their life and each bucket contains three categories:

1. **Personal Bucket** – This is all about you and your growth.
   a. Health – this includes elements such as your vitality, energy, exercise, diet, stamina, sleep, etc.
   b. Personal growth – this includes learning, developing new skills, reading, etc.
   c. Experiences & memories – this includes creating special moments for yourself, for the people around you and taking time to enjoy life.

2. **Relationship Bucket** – This is all about your connection with your family and friends.
   a. Your wife – this includes the passion, love, respect, sex, evolution, etc. in your marriage; being the best husband you can be.
   b. Your kids – this includes loving, teaching, protecting, spending time with your kids; being the best father you can be.
   c. Your friends and family – this includes your extended family, friends and the people you love.

3. **Wealth Bucket** – This concerns adding prosperity and abundance to your life.
   a. Career/Business – this includes your job or your business.
   b. Finances – this includes the money you make as well as other investments.
   c. Contribution – This includes giving back to others in ways of love, time, energy, monetary funds, service, or mentorship.

Right now, your goals may be skewed to one bucket. Having more balance will increase your fulfillment in life. Having one goal for each category in each bucket gives you nine goals in total. Chunking them in three's, they're easy to manage.

SMART Goals

Goals should be SMART, which is an acronym:

Specific – Make your goals as specific as you can e.g. My wife and I have sex three times a day.

Measurable – Ensure that your goals are easy to measure. The tougher they are to measure, the tougher it is to keep on track.

Attractive – Set goals that get you fired up e.g. My wife and I have crazy sex three times a day!

Realistic – Ensure your goals are realistic meaning that you don't need a magic genie to attain them. Having a goal like my wife and I have sex 43 times a day, every day, may not be realistic unless you have nothing else to do during the day.

Timely – Put a deadline on your goals, and I recommend 90 days. If you're goal is to have sex seven times a day 12 months from now, and you're only having sex seven times in an entire year right now, that might feel out of your reach. But going from where you are to three times a day in 90-days is inspiring to say the least!

State your goals in the present tense. You want to trick your mind. You want to think, act, and feel that your goal is already achieved. Which comes first, becoming a millionaire or having a millionaire's mindset? Unless you win the lottery, having the millionaire mindset precedes making millions.

Faith and belief is critical to goal achievement. If you're not acting on your goals, it could be because you don't really believe you can reach them. You've set yourself up for failure before you've even begun.

Lots of men are afraid to set goals because they would have to hold themselves accountable. So break your goals down into smaller units that are more easily achievable. But goals do need to challenge you. If you don't feel any resistance, you'll likely lose motivation over time. Challenge creates growth, and it's growth that keeps you inspired. Looking back at the obstacles you've overcome gives you motivation to keep going.

Three Types of Goals

It may seem like goals are simply goals, but there are three distinct types of goals:

1. **Outcome-focused goal** – This type of goal outlines the end result you are looking for. "I am the winner of the Boston Marathon.".
2. **Performance-focused goal** – This type of goal outlines the level of performance you want to achieve. "I ran the Boston Marathon in 2:02."
3. **Process-focused goal** – This type of goal defines the system you want to achieve. "I run 15 miles three times a week."

It's important to know the differences between the three types of goals. For example, you may have an outcome goal too soon without having a process goal in place. Or you might have a process goal, when you should be focused more on an outcome. If you're one of those guys who likes details, you can break your goals down into all three.

Prioritize Your Goals

If life was perfect and you had unlimited resources (time, money, energy, passion, etc.), you wouldn't have to worry about prioritizing. But that's not the reality. Prioritizing your goals allows you to adjust to the ups and downs of your life. You may be in an upswing where life is great and you have a ton of time and money to do what you want, or you could be in a downswing where your time is being squeezed and you're having other challenges in life. Prioritization allows you to allocate your resources appropriately, so your goals aren't conflicting with each other.

As I'm writing this, I have other projects but my number two goal overall is to finish the book. Spending quality time with my family is number one. All my goals are important but they're just not vital to me at this time. I feel clear about this. You should be very clear on how you structure your days and time. Clarity in your calendar creates clarity in your mind and emotions. This clarity is what you need to reach your goals.

Top of Mind

It can be easy to get off track on your goals. A key employee might leave your business or an unexpected expense could come up. Something could catch your attention and you start going down a different path.

I call these distractions the squirrel syndrome and I'm personally prone to it myself. I need to consciously keep myself on track because my mind goes in different directions at once. That's why writing down your goals and keeping them visible throughout the day is a great way to keep you on track. Put them on your phone, put them up in your office, on your fridge, or anywhere else that's impossible to ignore.

Clarity

The single most important reason to have goals is to provide clarity. Goals are the alpha (beginning) of everything you create in your business or life. Studies have shown that goal setting can actually change the structure of your brain. One study in particular showed that multiple sclerosis patients who set ambitious wellness goals had fewer and less severe symptoms than a control group. Goal-setting actually helped heal their brains.

One of the biggest challenges you may face is not knowing which direction you want to go. This is very common for men. You may have the drive and be fully capable of getting a job done, but you may not be sure which job it is.

Your goals may not even be your own goals and that could be causing confusion in your life. Chris was a sales professional I came across several years ago. He was being mentored by a very prominent social media influencer. He was struggling to make progress in his sales role even though he was driven and intelligent. He had everything going for him.

But the one thing he lacked was clarity. The life he wanted to live was not the same life his fiancé wanted to live. He was hustling and grinding to provide her an extravagant lifestyle. He absolutely loved her but he felt like he had to be making significantly more money to please her.

They had met at one of his mentor's conferences for sales professionals who wanted to make a lot more money. They eventually fell in love, and shortly thereafter he realized that he didn't want to be stressed for the rest of his life. He wanted to settle down but she wanted to do more travelling and partying. He was conflicted internally and didn't have the clarity he needed.

After a few of our conversations, he realigned his goals to the ones he really desired. He said he didn't feel like a fraud anymore. She ended up leaving him for someone else but that was too bad for her. Chris went on to start his own business and doubled what he was making in his sales role in less than a year. I guess she missed out.

Before you write down your goals, ask yourself this question: "Why do I want to achieve this goal?" Good reasons lead to good goals. Great reasons lead to premium goals.

Summary Action Items

1. Create your vision for your future life.

2. Create three SMART goals for each bucket: personal, relationships and wealth.

3. Ensure that your goals get you fired up.

4. Determine if you need outcome, performance or process goals.

5. Be clear about your goals and prioritize them.

6. Keep your goals at the top of your mind.

CHAPTER THREE

Your Identity

"Your identity is like your shadow: not always visible and yet always present."

-Fausto Cercignani

A couple of months after leaving my executive career, I wondered if I had thrown my entire life away. All of those years of working my butt off to climb the corporate ladder only to end at square one. In the corporate world I was somebody, an executive with a great reputation and I was close to the top of the food chain. Starting my consulting and coaching firm felt like I was at the very bottom.

I compared myself to top consultants and coaches in the industry like Tony Robbins, Robin Sharma, and Dan Sullivan. They had thousands and even millions of followers and I had a few hundred. I felt like I was starting from scratch again.

I felt useless and lost a good chunk of my self-confidence. But I couldn't wallow in self-pity forever because I had a family to take care of. I even physically slapped myself in the face a few times trying to knock myself out of it. The worst part of it was that I felt like a hypocrite. I was supposed to be the guy who coached other men out of these situations, and now I was in one myself.

Strangely enough, I was the same guy, who a few months ago,

was full of confidence. Why was I feeling such a disparity between then and now?

It was because of how I looked at myself. There was a change in my identity. I had viewed myself as the "go to guy," a successful executive who got the job done. I was assigned to almost every major project because of my expertise, skill, and tenacity. Now my perception of myself was becoming radically different and that was holding me back.

When I started to understand this, I shifted my identity to that of a successful entrepreneur on a mission to help others. Almost immediately, the transformation was like night and day. In a couple of weeks, I landed one of my biggest clients.

What is Identity?

Identity is defined as "the distinguishing character or personality of an individual." Your identity is how you perceive that "distinguishing character or personality," and that perception determines how you behave. Your identity is an "I am...." statement, and it can be very convincing.

If you believe that your identity is that of an introvert (e.g. "I am an introvert"), you'll shy away from meeting new people at a party. If you had a couple of drinks, you might let go of that part of your identity and be a lot more social.

Identity is the foundation of everything you do from the moment you wake up to the moment you go to bed. It's always there, like a shadow. It influences your thoughts and emotions. When you give yourself an identity, your mind will do everything it can to stay within those boundaries. Trying to remain consistent with your identity can be a lot of work if the identity isn't aligned with your goals.

Create Your Identity

If I asked you about your identity, would you be able to accurately describe it in a few short sentences? You might say something like, "I'm a husband, father, mortgage broker and I like to play golf."

These are roles that you have, but your identity is more than your roles. You must go deeper and find the very essence of your soul. Men can do amazing things when they go beyond the limits that the average man puts on himself. Identity is the only difference between you and that guy who has the life he wants.

Don't worry about who you are right now. Figure out who you need to be in order to achieve your goals. Your current identity was created through years of experiencing the life you lived. The way you grew up, how you were parented, the way your friends and colleagues treated you and the list goes on. Your current identity is a culmination of years of environmental stimuli and your own internal thoughts and emotions. You were molded into who you are now which means that you can mold yourself into who you want to be. So now you can create your own identity.

You're probably thinking one of three things:
- I can't change my identity
- If I change my identity, I'll be a fake
- I'm ready to change my identity, just tell me what to do.

First, you can change your identity. Elon Musk wasn't born a brilliant innovator, he created his identity himself. If you met Elon when he was five, you probably wouldn't have thought that he would be one of the world's most foremost influencers.

Second, changing your identity doesn't mean you're a fake. Do you behave the same way with your children that you do with your employees? No, you switch your identity based on your situation. That does not make you a fake.

Third, if you're ready to change, keep reading. By taking control of your identity you are taking control of your destiny. Instead of others molding you into who they want you to be, you get to mold yourself into who you want to be.

Your Core Identity

Just as a mango has a seed at its core, you have a core in your identity. That core is surrounded by a more fluid identity. Certain parts of your identity remain constant or fixed in almost every situation that you're in. The more fluid part of your identity can easily change based on your situation.

I'll give you a sneak peek into my core identity, which has three elements: "I am a leader, a learner, and a positive teacher."

My entire life revolves around this identity. The learning and teaching part came naturally to me. I have an unparalleled drive for both, and I have no idea where it came from. Maybe from my great grandfather who was a spiritual and religious teacher for 50 years. Talent and skill can travel from one generation to the next through energy passed down from genes. If your children have amazed you in some way and you wonder where they got that talent from, it could be from a previous generation. The leader element of my identity was not natural at all for me. I had to build on it for years for it to become part of my core identity.

Everything I do in life is based on these three elements from how I raise my children to how I operate in business.

Who are you at the very core of your being? What characteristics does your core identity need to have? When you are clear about your core identity, everything else falls into place. You have more confidence, certainty, control and many of the other C's that come along with being The Complete Man.

You may be wondering how long it takes to change your identity. It really depends on you. How badly do you want to change it? How much effort are you willing to put in? How committed are you to overcoming the challenges you face in creating your new identity? You can change your identity overnight if you truly want to. I witness men do it almost every day.

For a quick guide to creating a powerful core identity, go to www.completemanbook.com/resources.

Your Values

What you value determines how you make decisions and act. Your actions then influence your identity. When you have strong values, you have a stronger identity.

It's important to create a list of your top ten values. Write down your definition of each value so it is crystal clear. Also write down how your life will be impacted if you don't live up to your values.

You may discover that you have conflicting values. I coached a very wealthy and successful gentleman who placed independence and family at the top of his list. He would travel by himself and leave his family at home. He couldn't figure out why his wife and kids were feeling abandoned. He enjoyed travelling on his own because he valued independence. He also enjoyed spending time with them when he returned. He didn't realize that his values were conflicted. After some coaching, he moved independence further down on the list and he ended up traveling more with his family.

Be honest with yourself when you write down your values. You may write down a value but not actually be living up to it at all. All men want to live to good values but the question is do they really? The good news is that you can change your values. After you've written down your current values, write down the values you need to develop in order to achieve your goals in life.

Your Fluid Identity

Fluid identity is fun to play around with. You can create multiple identities based on your goals or the situations that you're in. When I have quality time with my kids, my fluid identity is Disney Dad. I try to create moments for them that they will enjoy and remember for years. It's fun for them and it's fun for me.

Am I always Disney Dad? No. Sometimes I have to be more disciplinary and Disney Dad goes out the window. I have multiple identities with my wife. I may need to be an erotic lover one day and an attentive supporter another. The more versatile you can be, the better your relationships will be as well.

When your identity is too rigid, not only does your life get boring but you also struggle with change. A lot of guys have problems in their marriage because they can't shift into another identity. The same approach to different situations doesn't always work. In fact, it rarely works.

It may feel odd at first when you use different identities for different situations. You may feel like you're acting, and it's not real. But it becomes as real as you make it. Have you ever come across a man who behaves the exact same way in every situation he's in? Nothing about them changes at all. According to Mark Leary, Ph.D. professor of Neuroscience and Psychology at Duke University, that could be considered a personality disorder. Having multiple and fluid identities is very healthy.

Layers of Your Identity

Based on his research, Professor Leary found that people's identities typically fall into five categories. Knowing these categories can give you a stronger understanding of how you see yourself and operate.

1. **Physical or biologic** – characteristics such as race, gender, height or weight.
2. **Personality** – characteristics such as being funny, charming, or tough.
3. **Social relationships** – these could include being a father, son or husband.
4. **Social groups** – including clubs, teams, or citizenship in a country.
5. **Transcendental** – seeing yourself as a spiritual being, a form of energy, or a child of God.

Now that you're aware of the different aspects of identity, you'll see patterns within your own identity as well as in others around you. Some people associate their identity more to social groups rather than as individuals. Men in the U.S. often identify themselves as Republicans or Democrats, rather than as citizens of the U.S. You emphasize certain aspects of your identity based on your personal experience.

Protect Your Identity

If you don't create your identity and protect it, others will create it for you. Humans by nature are creatures of opinions and judgements. It only takes a fraction of a second for the human brain to form an opinion of another. Who you associate with matters. If you're trying to enhance your identity and others around you aren't supporting you, you may have to change your environment.

If you're currently overweight and you want the identity of being a fit person, then you need to hang around with people who have a similar identity or will at least support your identity. If you need to eat healthy but your wife is feeding you junk food, you need to either ask her to make you something healthier or make it yourself.

Be cautious on what you project on others too. You can easily influence someone else's identity. You can change how a person sees himself or herself just by the words you say. That's why I'm extremely careful about how I talk to my children. Instead of saying, "You're messy" I say, "You're making a mess." This way I'm speaking about the behavior rather than their identity. I had to undo many of the old elements of my identity that my parents had placed on me. I don't blame them; they had no clue how their words impacted me. Many of the components were good, and some weren't so good. People are extremely vulnerable to this influence so I ask that you be conscious and aware of your impact.

Ego

Ego is a word that refers to a person's sense of self-esteem or self-confidence, and also a sense of separation from others. Ego and identity are in some respects similar. The moment you see yourself as separate and unique from others, you have formed an identity which is ego-based.

When your ego takes control of you, it becomes a detriment to your well-being and growth. Spiritual teachers frown on ego because it goes against the concept that we are all essentially one. If you're a pro athlete and so focused on it that it impacts other areas of your personal happiness, perhaps your ego has taken control. In my opinion, when your identity controls you, it becomes ego. When you control your identity, it's truly you.

It bothers me when ego is seen as the root of selfishness. Many spiritual teachers will tell you this. I don't believe ego is all bad. Pro athletes need to have an ego to be the best. Michael Jordan didn't walk onto the basketball court without an ego. Neither did Kobe Bryant or Lebron James. They all had an ego-based belief that they were the best. Ego allows people to move beyond the average and do great things. Keep your ego in check and it can help you do great things.

The Biggest Bang for Your Buck

If you're struggling to change your life and you don't know where to start or you're feeling overwhelmed and don't have the energy or time to execute everything in this book, focus on your identity. It's the most important element to living as The Complete Man.

The man you see in the mirror every day when you wake up is the man who makes things happen or does not makes things happen. How you perceive yourself, how you conduct yourself and how well you operate and perform is all based on your core identity. It's the core programming of your entire being. If someone gives you a magic wish, don't wish to have everything you want in life. Instead, wish to have the identity that will enable you to have everything you want in life. No one can take your identity away from you and having a powerful identity will get you through thick and thin regardless of what life throws at you.

Summary Action Items

1. Identify your current core identity. Determine how well it's serving you.

2. Go to www.completemanbook.com/resources to access the guide to creating a powerful core identity.

3. Write down your top 10 values and determine if they fit the life you want to have.

4. Identify the fluid identities that will enhance your quality of life and start living them.

5. Have an ego but keep it in check.

CHAPTER FOUR

Systems

"The average person using a great system can achieve amazing things."

-Purdeep Sangha

Dustin attended one of my workshops for entrepreneurs with his brother Adam. They were partners in an accounting firm, and each ran his own office in two separate cities. During the workshop, Dustin paid a lot more attention, took more notes, asked some really great questions, and seemed more engaged overall. Adam wasn't as attentive and I wondered if he only showed up because his brother made him.

At the end of the workshop, Dustin walked up to me and asked me some follow-up questions that he wasn't comfortable asking in front of the group. He and his brother were doing fairly well in their business. They knew they could still grow significantly, but neither of them were expert businessmen.

After I answered Dustin's questions, he asked if I would take him as a client. Then Adam joined our conversation and I asked if he would participate in the project to grow the business. I thought it was only natural as they were partners in the firm. But Adam said he could handle that on his own.

I later told Dustin that since they were partners, it would be best if Adam was on board. Dustin said, "He'll come around."

After working with Dustin for nine months, his office was gaining significant traction. His team was performing better, they were getting more clients, and revenues were increasing at the pace we had targeted. Adam's office was also growing but at half the pace.

Even though Dustin and Adam were brothers and partners, they were very competitive with each other. Brothers can be like that. I think Dustin wanted to teach Adam a lesson because he didn't share a single item about our strategy with Adam. Eventually, Adam reached out directly to me and asked me what I had been doing with Dustin for him to have grown his office that fast. I told him, "It's simple, we used a system."

Find the Clues

You can do it the hard way or you can do it the easy way. Adversity and challenges will force you to grow, develop new skills, habits, and talents. But if you have a goal in mind, the best way to achieve it is to figure out how others before you have done so.

The best CEO's analyze and study great CEO's. The best entrepreneurs study other entrepreneurs and their strategies. There is no shame in taking ideas from the greats.

Tony Robbins has a brilliant quote: "Success leaves clues." Once you find the clues, bring them together to create your own system. Anyone can achieve by accident. There are lots of one hit wonders who were just in the right place at the right time. It's difficult for them to recreate their success because they have no system. Find the people who have repeated success, because they have a system that can be replicated. Once you have a system of your own, you can repeat it to get similar results over and over again. Keep in mind that the system isn't foolproof and always needs to evolve and be updated.

I was able to outpace my colleagues in the corporate world

because I use a system that combines clues from many different disciplines. I combined neuroscience, performance psychology, spirituality and business practices. Having a background in science, I'm accustomed to experimenting, testing, failing, and eventually getting results.

I use myself as a guinea pig. For example, I'm an ardent planner. I schedule each day in an upcoming week. I once experimented with not making plans for six months. When I reviewed the results, I saw that I was almost twice as productive if I planned my weeks and days. It was eye-opening for me to see that impact.

Patterns

What patterns do you see in the men who have achieved what you want to achieve? What are the common elements? The Complete Men I work with have similar patterns. They all wake up relatively early and have a morning routine that includes meditation, exercising, and reading. They eat well and take care of their health and they put a high priority on their family.

Also watch out for the warning signs. One of the aspects of my life that I greatly reduced was my consumption of alcohol. I had been drinking since I was 17 and throughout my twenties. It wasn't destructive but I drank heavily on the weekends. Now, I measure my drinks and have a maximum of three to four ounces of spirits a week. Some weeks I don't drink at all. I never knew how not drinking as much would impact my health until I actually removed it from my routine. What patterns do you see in yourself that are sabotaging your progress? How are you getting in your own way?

Follow the Process

The universe is not completely random. Research shows that consistent processes are taking place everywhere you look. One of my consulting areas is business innovation. To be good at innovation, there is a process to follow. It's not about sitting in a room with others brainstorming and waiting for lightning to strike you with a brilliant idea.

Once you've identified your goal and the person you must become to achieve that completeness, then creating the process is the final piece to the achievement framework. A process is a series of steps that are followed to achieve a desired result. A system is a series of interconnected processes working together.

Consistency

Whatever you want to achieve, you must have a system and follow it consistently. Depending on the system, it can take days, weeks, months, or even years to accomplish your objective. The world is so focused on quick fixes, immediate gratification, and convenience, that men rarely have the patience to follow through. They assume that there is something wrong with the process so they move on to the next thing. I've been there myself and lost out on many opportunities. I missed some significant real estate returns because I didn't have the patience to follow the process.

I remember taking my first Tai Chi class. The instructor frustrated the heck out of me. He would tell us to ask questions when we had them. I once asked him a question about his perspective on Chi, the Chinese term for energy. He told me that I would have to practice for 15 years before he would answer that question for me. He taught me a great lesson that day. If I wasn't patient enough to stick with the process to see the results, I would never see the results.

Keep it Simple

The more complex your system is, the less likely you are to execute it. In the corporate world, I thought it was cool to use big words and look smart. As an entrepreneur, consultant, advisor, and coach, everything is about simplicity.

Simple means people can understand and don't get confused. There's no room for big words in the entrepreneur's world because by the time you finish saying the word, someone else has already beaten you to it. The simpler, the better.

It's All About Results

Your system must lead to results. If you're doing the activity and you're not seeing the results, you should determine if you're doing the right activities. You could be extremely hard-working, getting up early and staying up late, but if you're doing the wrong activities, you'll never hit your goals. I see men in the gym show up every day, do some funky workouts, and they still wonder why they aren't in shape. They have the heart and the will but they have the wrong system. The average person using a great system can achieve amazing things. A great person using a poor system will achieve much less.

Try writing down all your activities in a day. Then take a piece of paper and make three columns. On the far left, write down all the activities from which you can see quick and direct results; in the middle, write down the activities that you can see indirect or delayed results; and on the far right, list the activities that aren't leading to any results at all.

Let's say you want to have more sex with your wife. A direct activity could be giving her a massage which gets her in the mood and you end up doing it. (Hint: this works well.) An indirect activity could be holding her hand as you're walking. You may not get sex from it right away but it brings her closer to you so that when the time is right, it happens. But going drinking with your buddies will not get you sex with you wife.

Your goal should be to maximize the direct activities and reduce the activities that don't help you at all. The indirect activities could be maximized or reduced. Keeping track of your activities and results greatly helps identify what's working and what's not.

Priorities

Time, money, effort, and energy are all priorities. Where you choose to put your priorities determines your progress. If you're trying to start four businesses at once, chances are that all four are going to fall apart. There is always an opportunity cost with your actions.

Almost everything I do is aligned with my priorities. If it doesn't fit my priorities, I don't do it. It's so easy to get sidetracked that a step in the wrong direction can lead you down a rabbit hole that is tough to come back from.

This happens frequently in business. You see a new opportunity and don't want to miss out so you put time and energy into it only to find out that it was a complete waste. Now your business is that much further behind. Exploring new opportunities is a smart and a healthy thing to do but if it's constantly taking your attention away from your main priorities, think twice.

SARR

SARR is a simple formula I use with men to help them enhance their systems. It's a process that enables you to constantly evolve.

Strategize – identity your main outcome and outline your processes and system.
Act – do it!
Review – observe and analyze your results.
Are you getting closer to your goal or not?
Revise – change the system if needed to get better results.

Remember, your system must constantly evolve to stay relevant. What worked today may not work tomorrow.

Be Resourceful

As a young man, I believed that making money was for the rich people. After all, it was easier for them because you have to have money to make money, right? Wrong! Availability of resources comes from being resourceful, not from starting with the resources yourself.

If you're a business owner looking to expand but you don't have the money sitting in your bank account, you can always find capital elsewhere. You just have to be resourceful. It may require you to learn how to make a better sales pitch, but the money is out there. You just have to find it.

When you are building your system, avoid limitations based on your current resources. If you don't have access to what you need, find it. Again, it's about building a simple system. Instead of building a more complex system because you lack the resources, find the resources and get straight to the point.

Les owned a business that offered great service but he wasn't attracting the clients he needed. He had a complex and confusing sales strategy. I suggested, "Let's partner with a sales organization in your industry. Let them sell your product and service."

Les was hesitant at first but when he looked at the years he wasted with his cumbersome sales strategy, he knew it was the right decision. He just needed to be more resourceful.

When you limit your resourcefulness, you limit your success. The men at the top are there because they didn't take "no" for an answer. They found the resources somewhere.

The Power of Habits

Your habits will make you or break you. Habits are consistent behaviors. Your habits, therefore, define your identity and your identity reinforces your habits. You can determine a man's identity by looking at his habits and vice versa.

When the system you use to get results becomes a habit, your system and your goals are no longer separate. They become a part of your identity. It's like those amazing guitar players who can play at any place and any time, because the guitar is an extension of themselves. That's the power of habits.

Most of your habits are created unconsciously by your brain to conserve energy, so you have the capacity to make more complex decisions. Your brain consumes up to 20% of your caloric intake. This means that running your body and thinking consumes energy. Your brain tries to be as efficient as possible by creating habits.

Once you establish a pattern over a period of time, your brain automatically builds neural connections that get stronger and stronger. By performing the same activity over and over again, you are hard-wiring your brain to perform those activities without having to expend more energy than needed. That's when conscious activity becomes unconscious.

When you first learn to ride a bike, it requires a lot of conscious attention and energy. You're doing everything you can to stay on your bike and not fall over. After some practice, your brain automates the easier tasks like peddling and balancing so you have more energy to make the conscious choices, like the direction in which you want to go.

Studies show that the average person has habitualized up to 45% of the day. Imagine walking around half your day on autopilot. You're already doing it. Once a habit is formed, it's difficult to break because you've already created those connections in your brain. That's why addiction is so challenging for men to overcome. It's programmed into the brain.

Empowering vs. Disempowering Habits

I don't look at habits as good or bad. I prefer to think of them as empowering or disempowering. They either move you towards your goals or keep you away from your goals.

There can be a fine line between the two. An empowering habit like working out can easily become a disempowering habit if you end up working out excessively, taking enhancement drugs that hurt your health, or spending more time working out than with your kids.

The first step is to be aware of your habits. Start by taking an inventory, which requires attention and self-awareness. You may not recognize all your habits because you're not even aware of them. Ask your family members and friends to disclose habits they see in you, both the empowering and disempowering ones. You'll be shocked by what you'll learn!

Summary Action Items

1. Find the clues from other successful people and use them.

2. Outline the processes and systems you need to achieve your goals.

3. Keep your systems simple.

4. Be consistent.

5. Identify which of your activities are getting results and which aren't.

6. Enhance your systems using SARR: strategize, act, review and revise.

7. Find the resources even if you don't have them yourself.

8. Create more empowering habits and reduce your disempowering habits.

CHAPTER FIVE

Fear

"A coward dies a thousand times before his death, but the valiant taste of death but once."

-William Shakespeare

George was a successful professional with a good medical practice. He lived in a nice area, drove a nice car, and had a beautiful wife. I had known George for a while before I began working with him as his business coach. He was my friend first, who remained my friend when he also became a coaching client.

When George and his wife had their firstborn child, his life changed. I knew that George and his wife always had some complications in their relationship, and parenthood greatly amplified them.

George had hired me to help him grow his business. At first, he was enthusiastic about our strategies for doubling his revenues in 18 months. But within a few months of his son's birth, he seemed to lose motivation. His physical posture changed, he stopped working out, he was late to our meetings and he didn't execute the business improvements we had agreed upon.

Gradually, our conversations reverted from business to our longstanding friendship. I saw that George was badly stressed out. At home, besides sleepless nights tending to his child, his wife was putting all kinds of pressure on him. She was even threatening to leave with the baby. He lived in fear that, any day, his wife would walk out the door with his son.

George and I worked through different strategies to overcome his personal challenges, but the problems only got worse. I started taking this personally because my clients' success is my success. I really liked George. I don't like to see my friends in pain and he was in pain. The worst part was this: he was suffering not because he was forced to, but because he chose to.

One issue was driving George absolutely crazy. His wife wouldn't allow him to take his son to see his family, or to invite his family over. This was his wife's way of controlling him and showing her resentment for him.

He and I had several conversations about how he could handle this situation. George was a loving person, and having his son as part of his extended family was hugely important to him. Finally, he decided to take his son to visit the family by himself, or at least try to.

When I sent George a text asking how the visit went, I got a quick reply – but not from George. His wife had commandeered his phone and she asked me to stay out of their business.

I felt badly that lots of boundaries were being crossed in this situation. When I met with George, I let him know that I wasn't going to be involved in his family drama. I asked him if he was going to step up and take a stand for himself with his wife. I also said that I could no longer work with him as a coach unless he would face his fears head on.

George's response was to apologize for letting me down. I replied, "You're not letting me down. You're letting yourself, and maybe your son too. Don't teach him that he should submit to his fears."

That was the last time I saw George. I've sent text messages on his birthday and haven't heard back.

What is Fear?

Fear can force you to grow and make you stronger, or it can reduce you to feeling like a little boy. To become a Complete Man, you need to get your fears out of the way so that you can live a complete life. It's that simple, although simple isn't the same thing as easy.

Fear is biologically designed to create a distance between you and what is triggering your fear. In many situations that's a very useful mechanism. If a shark is coming toward you in the ocean, it's a good idea to create distance from the shark. If there is a real threat, you legitimately need to move away from the threat as fast as possible.

But what if there isn't a real threat? What if that's just the way, consciously or unconsciously, that you choose to respond? And a really scary thing about fear is how you can be afraid of something without even knowing why.

Fear is primarily organized in two parts of your brain. The amygdala, a structure in the brain that is responsible for processing memory, decision making and emotions. The second structure is the hippocampus which is a critical component for learning, memory encoding, memory consolidation, and spatial navigation. The amygdala and the hippocampus work together to register fear and place it in your short and long-term memory. The next time you come across the same trigger, it can be easily recognized. If you've been bitten by a dog, you'll be more wary of the next dog that walks by you.

But it's not a perfect system. Memories of fear aren't always accurate. You may experience fear when the actual trigger is confused. If the dog that bit you was a giant schnauzer, you might still be afraid of a dachshund. What you fear could be completely fabricated in your mind. If you're aware that fear is a prevalent concern in your life, keeping a "fear journal" can help. Identify what triggered your fear and how you responded. Then see whether the fear and the response were really justified. If not, next time you'll be ready to respond differently. When you are triggered, dig deep to find out what's really causing the fear. Is it really what you think it is? In most cases it won't be.

The key is to bring reason and logic into play. Otherwise, fear will remain mysterious and powerful. I began to realize this when I was a young boy. My father would sometimes drink beyond his limits, and he would become a different person, a person I feared. Although I couldn't understand why this transformation took place, I had to put aside my fear because I was the only person in the house who could calm him down.

I was the one who put him to bed and even slept beside him. I never knew why, but my presence calmed him. I would lay there ever so still for hours, not making a sound, not moving an inch, barely breathing. I was frightened the whole time, but my dad was perfectly serene. In some mysterious way, whatever malign energy that was within him got transferred to me and transformed into fear. Today, when my wife asks me why I rarely get stressed out, I think it's because I did all my stressing as a kid.

Managing Fear

Growing up on an orchard, I learned how to prune trees. It meant removing old, dead, and diseased branches and shaping the tree so that the next crop is more fruitful. You can use the same principle to prune your fears.

All fears fall into one or more of four categories. The first is loss. If you're a CEO and your organization isn't performing well, you may fear losing your job. If your marriage is on the rocks, you may fear losing your spouse and your children.

The second bucket is reduction, or becoming "smaller." If your annual bonus is reduced, your self-esteem may be diminished. If you can't run as fast or throw a ball as far as you once could, you may fear that you're getting old and weak.

A third category is "going without." The prospect of living without the love and passion you always wanted can be frightening. Or imagine working all the time, with no chance to do what you really want.

The last bucket is different. Instead of losing or not gaining what you want, it's about getting something you don't want. Perhaps you're afraid you'll get heart disease because your father had it. Or that you'll be given a project at work for which you're unprepared.

As another form of journaling, I encourage you to write down your fears to determine which categories they fall into.

One way or another, fear will always be present. How you react to fear will determine whether you can overcome it.

Benefits of Fear

Fear, like other emotions, can be a source of energy that you can channel. If you've suffered a heart attack and the fear of death motivates you to eat healthy and exercise, fear has become a positive motivator. Fear of losing your job can lead you to learn new skills and excel as a leader.

The Dalai Lama has a brilliant illustration of how he deals with fear and other unfavorable emotions. He asks fear to come in for a cup of tea and entertains fear. He learns from fear because fear is there to tell him something. Once he understands why fear is there, he asks fear to leave. It's a brilliant way of understanding fear, using it to learn and grow stronger.

You can imagine inviting fear in for a beer and having a good chat. There is always something to learn from fear and getting to the root cause. Then you can ask fear to leave. If fear returns on a continuous basis, just don't open the door.

What Men Fear the Most

Over the years, I have noted the most consistent fears that haunt men:

- Going through life not living to your full potential.
- Not achieving the success you wanted.
- Aiming too high and failing.
- Losing respect and status.
- Not being loved.
- Being alone and poor.
- Not being needed.
- Being judged by others.
- Not being able to provide the lifestyle you want for your family.
- Losing your children in a separation or divorce.
- Having some other man raise your kids.
- Looking incompetent.
- Making bad decisions.
- Failing while your peers are succeeding.
- Not performing well in bed.
- Letting others down.
- Not having a purpose or meaning in life.
- Fear of death, leaving loved ones behind.
- Fear of being forgotten.

Overcoming Fear

As the neuroscientist Joseph LeDoux discusses in his book *The Emotional Brain*, psychologists believe that you are born with two natural fears: the fear of falling and the fear of loud noises. Human beings gradually learn to fear many other things. But just as you can learn to fear, you can also learn to overcome your fear. There are four tactics I teach to help men do this.

First, dissociate yourself from the fear. Fear is a situation, it's not you. You're not afraid, you just feel afraid at times. You're not weak, you're just impacted by certain things more than others. Don't allow your fear to become a part of you. Separate it and dissociate yourself from it. Fear is a thing, it's not you.

Second, view the situation from a third-party perspective. Be an observer rather than a participant. Ask yourself, "What would a person I admire do in this situation? How would he or she feel about this?"

Third, put the fear at a distance visually. Your mind tends to replay things over and over again and creates scenarios up-close. The closer the images are, the greater the focus and the greater the focus, the greater the intensity. The more details you give to the fear, the more intense it becomes. Put the image as far away as possible so you can barely make it out. Eventually, just refuse to allow that image back into your head.

Fourth, if your fear continues, reduce the time period you allow for it. Schedule a time period during the day to feel the fear and once the time is up, let the fear go. Don't allow yourself any more time to feel it. Slowly reduce the time period over several days until you don't need it anymore.

The best way to face fear is head on. I've never met a man that regretted facing his fears. But I've met plenty who wish they would've faced their fears earlier on. Men slowly die inside because they allow the fears to overtake their dreams and ambitions. Stop and look at your fears directly in the eyes and you'll realize that you're just looking into your own eyes. It's not external, it's all within you and you've created your own fears or you've allowed someone else to create them for you. A thousand years ago, men feared dying in war to protect their families. Now men fear being criticized for not making enough money. It's funny how things have changed. Today is your day to put your fears to rest and reclaim your life.

Death

Fear of dying is human nature. Men fear death for two main reasons. First, there is the unknown of what happens after death. Do you go to heaven? Do you turn into a different form or energy? Are you reincarnated into another living being? All of these are unknowns, and unknowns translate into fear.

The second fear can be even greater than the fear of the unknown. It's not living life to your fullest potential, not enjoying life as much as you should've and not having quality moments with your loved ones. It's the fear of regret and is fully in your control. Imagine leaving this world being The Complete Man and living at your highest potential. When you leave this world, you would have nothing to regret.

Summary Action Items

1. Write down your most frequent fears. Which category do they fall into: losing, lessening, going without, getting something you don't want?

2. Be more present and don't allow future-focused fears to interrupt what you do now.

3. Understand what your fears are telling you. Know that most of them have been given to you by conditioning.

4. Dissociate yourself from your fears. Be an observer of your fears. Put your fears at a distance. Schedule a short time period to feel the fear and then let it pass.

5. Become The Complete Man so you have nothing to fear, even death.

CHAPTER SIX

The Role of Men

"If you're not a leader, you're a follower."
-Purdeep Sangha

Jim had a great business, was making a ton of money, and had a beautiful wife and kids. You could say that he had it all and he was even looking to purchase a new private jet. I thought he was doing pretty well until suddenly one day he called me and told me he had lost his family.

I asked him what had happened. He said that he and his wife had a falling out and he was now living with his parents. His kids don't talk to him anymore and he wasn't sure what he should do next.

"What exactly did you do?" I asked.

Jim wouldn't tell me, but whatever it was, it wasn't good. When I first met him, I sensed he was a great businessman but his leadership in his family needed some work. Many professional men end up in this situation, and it happens because of certain basic misunderstandings.

The <u>Mindful</u> Alpha Male

This chapter is meant to guide you through the foundation of our roles as men. Having a clear understanding of what it means to be a man is critical. Before you're an entrepreneur, CEO, athlete, or whoever you identify yourself as, you are a man first. When you are incomplete and not fulfilled, you're not in your masculine power. You lack clarity, confidence, certainty and control. Those who are unhappy and seem like they're in their masculine power are most likely faking it. Inside they really feel lost.

Living as a mindful alpha male is the foundation of The Complete Man. While the term "alpha male" has been associated with aggressive, controlling, and belligerent behavior, the mindful alpha male is a very different concept.

Alpha is the first letter of the ancient Greek alphabet. It's the beginning, the source. Whatever you seek in life starts with you first. Everything you have or don't have is dependent on you. You are the alpha male of your life. But that's not all.

Mindfulness means being fully aware of what you are doing and how it impacts you and the world around you. A mindful alpha male is a man who is completely aware of the effects and outcomes of all his actions. To become a mindful alpha male, you must carefully examine your intentions and aspirations to determine if they benefit you, your family, and your community.

You may have good intentions for yourself but the results may not be good for others. Before you act, you must be aware of the possible outcomes from different perspectives. To live a life of success and fulfillment, you need to be both mindful and an alpha.

Family Leadership

I had a gentleman ask me a question in one of my workshops: "Who would be the followers if every man became a leader?"

He was right, but here's what I asked him in return "What are the chances of every man becoming a leader?"

There will always be plenty of followers, and there's nothing wrong with being a follower in certain aspects of life. At work, you're expected to follow your manager; in sports, you follow your coach; growing up, you may follow your father or older brother.

But what about when you're not a kid anymore? Should a man be the leader of his family? In my opinion the answer is yes, but only if he's a mindful alpha male. I've had the opportunity to observe families and relationships very closely and I'm able to determine very quickly if the man is the head of the household. If I see that the man is not stepping up as the leader, I'm rarely surprised when a couple is having problems. If the kids are consistently misbehaving or have other challenges, I always look at the leadership style of the father.

In my experience working with men, a strong man raises a strong and healthy family. Your strength will determine the strength of your family for generations. The stories that my father told me about his father and grandfather shaped me into who I am today. The same can be true for your children and grandchildren.

Stepping Up in the Community

When COVID-19 hit North America and the quarantine was enforced, I saw two types of behavior in men. Some went out and hoarded food and guns. They went into total survival mode. These men were conventional alpha males.

I also saw men helping their friends, family members, neighbors, and people they didn't even know. They went into helping mode. These are the mindful alpha males.

A healthy community leads to healthier families, healthier economics, and healthier people in general. A man who is in survival mode, who is frustrated with life, and who is simply not fulfilled has a tough time giving support to others. There needs to come a point in time when a man recognizes that true joy comes from what you give to your family, your community, and to everyone around you.

It bugs the hell out of me when men talk about how national laws or politics need to change in order to make things better. Change starts at home first. Then real change can happen at the community level. We need to hold each other accountable and then we can hold those at the top accountable. Just imagine if every community in the US and Canada was taking care of itself, we wouldn't be looking so hard at the government and what politicians are doing.

Masculinity

Masculinity in Western culture is associated with strong, courageous, dominant, logical, combative, compulsive and aggressive behavior. In comparison, femininity in Western culture is associated with sensitivity, empathy, being social, caring, communicative, compassion and attentiveness. Yet all these qualities exist in men and women in differing degrees.

For men, a healthy balance of masculinity and femininity is needed to function and be happy. Finding the balance may be a challenge at first, but once you have it, it's life-changing. You may have to push yourself past your comfort zone and break the stereotypes given to masculinity and femininity. As you get closer to what feels right for you, you'll feel better about yourself and others will react to you more favorably as well.

There's been a debate for decades regarding gender differences and the role of genetics versus conditioning. I believe that men and women are "equals but not equal." Both deserve the same respect and opportunities. As a 2017 article in the journal *Sex Roles* discusses, men may be better at certain things than women and vice versa. For example, a study of "wayfinding competence" – the ability of a person to orient themselves in physical space and to navigate from place to place – showed that higher feminine personality traits led to poorer performance. It's absurd that society has gotten to a point where women and men are competing more than they are working together.

The topic of gender is contentious. Some experts propose that there is no biological or genetic support for gender roles. They argue that gender is a societal construct. I absolutely agree. Society has shaped gender and it's also shaped evolution. Over hundreds of thousands of years, biology has shaped society and society has shaped biology

An article entitled "Masculine Temperament and Secondary Sex Characteristics," in the journal of the American Psychological Association, discusses basic biological differences between males and females. At eight weeks, a fetal brain either produces more testosterone and develops into a male, or continues on to develop into a female brain. The biological differences between a male brain and a female brain determine how a child will react to the environment as he or she is raised. For example, studies show that teenage boys can have up to 100 times more testosterone than girls.

Although having more testosterone might not cause greater aggression, it could allow boys to be more susceptible to aggression if they see it displayed by other boys. A study of fraternities found that the groups with higher testosterone had more unruly and wild behavior. Having more testosterone could encourage boys to be more easily influenced by aggression than girls.

The Need for Masculinity

Masculinity is amazing. Yet we have movements on how "toxic" it is. Masculinity is no more toxic than femininity. Both are essential to life. Similar to the term alpha male, masculinity has been confused with abuse, sexism and wrongdoing. A man who abuses women doesn't do it because of his masculinity, he does it because he's got tendencies to abuse and lacks values and control.

The negative impact of smothering masculinity is that we're raising neutral children. New generations that don't know what it means to be a man or a woman. If you ask a man nowadays to describe what it means to be masculine, he'll have a hard time telling you. Either that, or he'll be hesitant to express his opinions which is even worse.

Suppressing masculinity is the equivalent of shaking a pop can and throwing it against the wall. It's going to explode at some point. When you tell a man to bottle up his natural instincts, it's dangerous. His pent-up feelings will eventually come up and sometimes at the wrong times. That's why sports, exercise, boxing, and other forms of releasing this energy is important for good health. We have a lot of angry men and boys because we're telling them not to be masculine. This eventually comes out in forms of resentment, depression, anger and violence. A majority of violent crimes are committed by men. We need to teach these men how to use their masculinity to live a better life and not resort to tactics that hurt themselves and others.

Be masculine, it's great. Your wife needs it, your children need it and your community needs it. You don't need to have a chest full of hair and bash it like a gorilla. Be aware of the degree of your masculinity and where it needs to be enhanced or toned down. For example, my wife prefers when I take control and am dominant, especially behind closed doors. I can feel us drifting apart when my dominance is lowered.

Masculinity isn't facing a problem; it's facing an extinction. Those who are impacted most are women and the children. They need strong men to live happy lives. Some women may tell you differently but speak to a feminine woman who is with a strong man. She'll tell you how much she appreciates the masculinity in her husband.

Turning this ship around isn't going to be easy. There are a lot of things going against men. First, men who deliberately hurt others, should be held accountable. Lack of consequences has allowed men to act immorally. Integrity should be something that all men live by. We need to walk the talk so our children understand that if we say something, we mean it and we do it. That way they grow up with integrity.

Men must live with values and principles. If I asked you for ten values that you live by, would you be able to easily list them? Do you live by those consistently? Is your word your bond? My grandfather made sure that I understood that when a man says something, he better do it and stick with his commitments.

Women shouldn't have to hold us accountable for immoral actions, we should be able to do that ourselves. Instead of shifting responsibility to others, we must take on the responsibility. Instead of thinking of "me", we must think of "we." Stand up for what you believe in even if you are afraid of retribution. That's what we do as men. We are here to serve and protect before all else. I say this in most of my workshops "we are the last line of defense". The next generation won't understand what it means to be men unless we step up to show them.

The Importance of Mentorship

Looking back at my life, I'm so blessed to have had amazing mentors. Most of them weren't famous, highly educated, or very wealthy. They were everyday men with big hearts and wisdom.

My grandfather was one of them. He spent 30 years in the British-Indian army and he was the most spiritual and most masculine man I knew. He was disciplined, yet very empathic. He blended two worlds together: the world of war and the world of spirituality. It was an odd mix that taught me so much about life. I was 19 when he passed away and I wish I would've spent more time learning from him.

So many men are just lost. They're easily influenced by the media, they're disconnected from life and they're looking up to men who aren't the best role models. They're chasing the dollar, the fame, the status that are fun to have, but don't really bring fulfillment. They're getting caught in a rat-race life, and who's suffering as a result? It's not just the men. It's also their wives, children and other family members.

It's tough for guys to open up. I have conversations with several men each day and the biggest hurdle is getting them to reach out for help. They need a different perspective and strategy on how to approach whatever is getting in their way.

My grandfather would say, "There is no pride in suffering." Men who need help should seek out mentors and men who are in a position to help others should seek out mentees. Men lose their way because they don't have someone there to guide them in the right direction.

I have set aside hours each week to help men *pro bono* not because it makes me feel good but because it's my duty. I owe it to my mentors to give back to others what my mentors gave to me.

Be the MVP of Your Life

When my dad walked into the room, I wouldn't even have to see him, I could feel that he was there. His presence and energy was powerful and calming. My dad was a police officer in India and learned how to be disciplined, presentable and have presence. Our family and friends still talk about his presence to this day. As I'm typing out this chapter, a few tears come to my eyes. I truly miss him and his presence. If your father had that same presence, you know what I'm talking about. If it wasn't your father, I'm sure there is someone else in your life who had an equivalent impact on you.

Today power is frowned upon. Power is associated with abuse, neglect, and control. But that's not what power is. Power is the ability to influence your environment in the direction you want. The main reason why men feel depressed or fearful is because they feel powerless. They feel that some element of their life, their work, their marriage, their financial situation, or other area is controlling them. Wet noodles get thrown against a wall to see if they stick. Often they don't, and they lose their drive, conviction and meaning. They become even softer and weaker.

Stand up and reclaim your power. When you take back power, you know that regardless of what happens around you, you'll be able to get through it and be successful. Nothing has greater presence than a man in his power. He doesn't have to say a word, you can just feel it. It's a form of energy that radiates. Embrace your power and step into it.

Who's the most valuable player in your life? It should be you. You are the captain of your team. You are the one who makes and executes the plays. You are your biggest investment. To get to where you want to be in life, be the MVP who attracts it. There are men who win and there are men who lose. The only difference is that the ones who win become the alphas and create their lives while others choose to live with what's handed to them. You get to choose which team you want to be on.

Summary Action Items

1. Be a leader and a mindful alpha male.

2. Embrace your masculinity and power.

3. Be the leader of your family.

4. Stand up against poor leadership.

5. Contribute to your community.

6. Be a mentor and role model for men.

7. Be the MVP of your life.

CHAPTER SEVEN

Your Intimate Relationship

"One word frees us from all the weight and pain of life. That word is love. "

-Sophocles

In 2016, I dated Sara, a girl in high school who I totally fell for. She had recently moved into our small city of Kelowna. I had never seriously dated anyone until I met her and for some reason we just fell in love.

Being Indian (as in Indo-Canadian), we were both forbidden by our parents from dating. We were not allowed to hang out privately at all. Her father was a general contractor and was building a home for us until we found out that he was fraudulently creating credit cards and loans under my dad's identity. He was also stealing supplies from the construction site. Her father had a drug addiction and he had to pay for it somehow. When my parents found out what he had done, they were absolutely furious.

Oh shit! Now I've fallen in love with a girl who I shouldn't be dating and on top of that, my parents hated her family's guts. It was a total romance story and I could make a movie about it because we dated for eight years, most of which were secret from my parents and hers.

I hated lying to my parents. I felt that constant fear of what would happen if they found out. How would they react? What would they say? I never wanted to disappoint them because they worked so hard to give my brother and I the best life they could.

The day came that I told them that I wanted to marry Sara, and they stopped talking to me for about six months. I didn't really blame them. In our culture, reputation is a big thing. My parents were one of the original Indian families in Kelowna and it was important for my parents to uphold their reputation. Her family had a bad rep and my parents wanted nothing to do with it. But eventually they came around and agreed half-heartedly.

Throughout the years, my fiancé and I had gone through many trials. We never really had the guidance that kids should have from their parents about relationships. Her role models were her parents, and her parents had a poor relationship. My parents loved each other but my dad's drinking kept pushing them apart. So she and I lacked the skills to have a healthy relationship.

We loved each other but that wasn't enough. We didn't know how to work with each other in the relationship to give each other what we needed.

Long story short, by the time we got married, our relationship had fallen apart. We probably shouldn't have gotten married in the first place. It lasted only four months. We loved each other but we were not right for each other. We had been together since high school and we had become two people with different needs, interests and desires.

After we split up, I went on a quest to find out why relationships work or fail. Why are some couples madly in love for many years, while others can barely get along? I spent the next few years studying the psychology of relationships.

Here's the irony. Part way through my relationship with Sara, we had split up for a year because she was having a fling with my best friend's brother-in-law. When I found out, I was shattered but brought myself together and realized that I wasn't giving her something she needed. I never held a grudge against her or him. Ruby still asks me to this day, why I don't hold a grudge against him. First, my dad always taught me to never hold a grudge. It's not worth it. Second, this guy introduced me to Ruby. My best friend was in town for the weekend and brought his brother-in-law. This guy had met Ruby previously and thought we should get to know each other so he introduced us. I tell my wife that had the events not gone as they did, I wouldn't have met her. How ironic that the guy who added issues in my past relationship is the same guy who would introduce me to my current wife. Sounds like something from a soap opera.

Four years after Sara and I split up, I met Ruby, my present wife. When I met Ruby, I thought our connection would go no-where fast. She was a city gal and I was a small-town farm boy who moved to the city. I lived a simple life and she liked to live a fancier life. She liked brand names, and I couldn't care less. I liked going to pubs and she liked fancy restaurants. I loved animals and nature and she loved malls and spas. We were polar opposites, and I believe that's why we've always been attracted to each other. We bring two different worlds together.

It's not always easy though. We were even separated for a short period. During that time, Ruby found out she was pregnant and she didn't tell me immediately. When she eventually told me, we made an effort to come back together.

We've gone through family dramas, financial challenges, differing opinions on where to live, how we want to educate our children, and much more. We're just like every other couple who strive to make marriage a relationship that we both want to be a part of, not something that we are forced to be a part of.

We continue to have our ups and downs but they're less frequent and less intense. As much as I've learned about relationships, I'm still continuously learning about Ruby and about myself. My relationship with Ruby and our two children is one of the most fulfilling aspects of my life. Still, I know I could spend many more years learning about relationships and still not have all the answers.

Your Relationship Is a Reflection of You

Over the years, I've observed that men who are in healthier relationships perform better in all areas of life. I've also seen men in bad relationships who, as a result, seem completely defeated. It's not that they don't want to have a good relationship. They just don't know what to do because they feel like they have already tried their best.

But I'm a firm believer that "the grass is always greener when you water it." You are accountable for your own happiness. Jack Canfield once told me something that I will never forget. He talked about a man being 100% accountable for every aspect of his life. If he leaves even a fraction of accountability to someone else, he is giving up the power to create the life he wants.

Great relationships aren't fairy tales. They really exist. They just require work – your work. As a Complete Man, you must accept that complete accountability.

Love and Give

The reality is that you are happy with your relationship or you're not. It's as simple as that. The two things you need to ask yourself are: 1) Are you being the best husband, lover, father, leader and man you can be? 2) Are you settling in your relationship?

Most men get into a relationship to receive. They want to receive love, receive comfort, receive sex, and much more. But a great relationship is based on giving. When you give your wife everything you can and your wife gives you everything she can, it becomes a beautiful union.

Men are built to solve problems and fix things, but that can be dangerous in a relationship. With your partner, your job isn't to be the problem solver all the time. Your job is to just love her for who she is. Don't try to turn her into a version of yourself. You want her to compliment you, not be you. She operates on a very different software system. She doesn't need to be fixed and she doesn't need to be improved.

Ask and you shall receive. If you want something in your relationship, you must ask for it. It's easy to assume that your wife is a mind-reader but she's not. Yes, women have amazing intuition but they're not psychics. "Well my wife should know me by now" is what I hear. No, she shouldn't. If you want better sex, ask for it. If you want your wife to get off of your back about something, ask her to. It's your responsibility to ask. If you ask and she doesn't deliver, that's a different story.

A relationship can become imbalanced if one person is continuously giving and the other is continuously taking. If you are continuously giving and you're not getting much in return, you will very likely become resentful. Regarding this, my wife and I practice a simple technique. Each day we ask each other, "What is the one thing you most need from me today?" It's easy to deliver because it's just one thing. We don't make it complicated by creating a laundry list of needs.

What do you give to your relationship? The more each person gives, the more fruitful the overall relationship. You wouldn't walk into the office, put your feet up on the desk and do nothing. You need to add value to the organization. The same goes for your relationship. The more value you give, the better your relationship will be. Value can be many different things from providing emotional support, financial security to bringing humor into the relationship.

Here are the three most important things that a woman wants a man to give to a relationship:

1. **Safety & security** – A woman wants you to provide a safe environment in which she can be herself. But don't confuse safety with a lack of excitement. She also wants to be with a man who can provide for her and the family. She wants to be with someone who can take care of her.
2. **Understanding** – A woman wants to be understood, not improved or corrected. When she's unsure of her own feelings, she just wants you to be there for her.
3. **Presence** – A woman wants you to give her your total and undivided attention. She wants you to be present with her in mind, body, and soul.

And the top three things that men value in women:

1. **Freedom** – A man wants a woman who can give him space to do what he wants and what he believes he has to do.
2. **Respect** – A man wants to be with a woman who will respect him for who he is and the hard work and effort he puts into providing for his family.
3. **Sex** – A man wants to be with a woman who will satisfy his sexual desires.

What Women Really Want

You've heard the rumors that women want sensitive men, and that's true. Women are attracted to men who are able to show and share their emotions. A Complete Man is confident and is able to show his emotions. Women are attracted to mindful alpha males. They can sense when a man is a leader and knows what he wants. They also know when a man is kind and looks after others.

He can take charge but also wears his heart on his sleeve. They want both.

I dated one woman who taught me a valuable lesson. After dating for a few months, she literally told me that she wanted to be with a man who takes charge. She wanted me to "dominate" her, but not in a controlling way. She wanted to be respected and she also wanted me to take the lead in our relationship. I thought she was unique but I gave it a try. I stepped up my masculinity and she loved it. Going forward, I thought things would be different with other women but I was wrong. They wanted a man who took charge. Finally, I said to myself, "Okay, I get it." If you're still not convinced, looking at the sales of *Fifty Shades of Grey* may help. It's the hottest selling novel for women.

I'm convinced that in most relationships where the woman takes the lead, the man could not feel complete. This is a generalization, but I do see this pattern as I work with men every day.

The Basics of Attraction

A man and woman are attracted to each other because they are opposites. This goes beyond just sexual attraction and into the realm of desiring one another spiritually. There are two different energies that pull towards each other like the two ends of a magnet. In the Chinese culture, this is described as Yin and Yang energies, and in Indian it's Yoni and Linga. They're opposite energies that come together in perfect unity. In Western culture, these polarities are referred to as masculine and feminine.

One energy is not better than the other. They both have their strengths and there is no lack in either. If you had a monster truck and a Ferrari, both with 1000 horsepower, one would not be better or weaker than the other. You would use each accordingly to its function. You would use the monster truck for off-road travel and the Ferrari for highway travel. They are both powerful in their own ways.

Masculine	Feminine
Wants freedom	Wants to be owned
Minimizes	Makes small thing big
Solid/certain	Expansive
Calm/still	Flowing
Forgets/empties	Holds on/fills up
Goal oriented	Connection oriented
Task focused	Creative
Wants peace	Wants variety
Dominating	Absorbing
Desires appreciation	Desires praise

Energy Imbalance

Sometimes in relationships, the man takes on more feminine energy and his wife reacts by elevating her masculinity. This may happen when the woman is the sole breadwinner and the man is at home. Consequently, the husband will lose his drive and his attraction for his wife. Or the wife will lose her attraction for her husband because she needs someone who has more masculine energy than herself.

My wife and I separated because I had allowed this imbalance to happen. The moment I stepped back into my masculine state, she shifted back into her feminine. She felt more like a woman and I felt more like a man. We were attracted to each other once again.

Take a moment to observe your relationship. Where is your energy right now? Where is your wife's energy? Do you have that attraction? Again, it's beyond just sexual energy.

The upcoming generation is receiving mixed messages. Boys are being taught not to be masculine and girls are being taught to be more masculine than boys. Boys are learning to be more sensitive and passive (which is okay to a point) and girls are learning to be tougher than boys (which is okay to a point as well). But if it goes beyond a healthy threshold, we'll have an entire generation of men and women who have their energies reversed.

The Silent Killer

Resentment is a silent killer of relationships. Some couples harbor resentments for years, but their relationship will never work until they learn how to get over it. Like a cancer, it festers and grows until you can't handle it anymore.

The only way to get over resentment is to stop the behavior that causes it. Identify the root cause of the resentment, discuss how you and your wife can eliminate it and move on. Both parties must agree to put it to rest.

Resentment is a result of someone's needs not being met. If you're resenting your wife, identify what need you want to have met and ask her to meet it. If she's resenting you, find out what needs you're not meeting for her.

Cheating

In the majority of cases, people cheat because their needs are not being met by their partner. A terrible thing about cheating is the guilt that men carry, sometimes for the rest of their lives. I don't condone cheating but I do understand why men do it.

Below, in no particular order, are specific reasons why men cheat:

- Lack of sexual fulfilment
- The need to desire someone or the need to be desired
- Not being respected in your relationship
- Being controlled
- Not being accepted for being who you are
- Lack of emotional connection
- Lack of appreciation
- Lost the connection with your spouse

Some men are so loyal to their relationship that, rather than cheat, they live miserably for the rest of their lives. They won't cheat to satisfy their needs and they won't leave their relationship either. If you don't want to cheat but you want a better relationship, make it better. Be the best husband you can be for the next 90 days and also ask for what you need and want. If you don't see the progress you desire, make a choice. Accept things as they are or move on.

Communication

Communication is the second most important element to a successful relationship next to the attraction of complimentary energies. Communication is a form of influence. People communicate because they want the person receiving the message to do something, whether it's now or in the future.

Here are six elements for effective communication:

1. **The message** – What is the core message you want to deliver? Make it easy to understand.
2. **The medium** – What is the best channel to communicate the message? Is it in person, phone, text, email, video or other channels?
3. **The messenger** – What personality do you deliver the message in? Do you need to be compassionate, directive, loving, etc.?
4. **"We vs. me"** – How do you create a common ground with the person you're communicating with? Do you have a common background, common interests, or common goals?
5. **The timing** – What's the best time to communicate the message? Timing is everything. You can deliver the right message at the wrong time and it can bomb.
6. **Verify the understanding** – How will you confirm that they truly understood the message?

If you're having difficulty communicating, try to find a connection using common ground first. I find it makes difficult conversations a lot easier. Common ground could include: a common goal, common feeling, common belief, common background, common social group, common experiences or common memories.

Compromise

Compromise is rarely effective. Instead, find a solution you can both feel excited about. If I want to go on vacation somewhere hot and my wife wants to go somewhere cool, it doesn't make sense for us to find a place that is warm. I'd rather go somewhere cool this time so my wife is happy and I'll be happy because she's happy. Next time, go on a hot vacation.

Principles in Relationships

Creating principles in your relationship reminds you of what's important. Principles keep everyone on the same page. There are times when I behaved in ways that I'm not proud of. I'm a good person and I have a big heart so why am I doing this? It was because I would just forget and operate randomly. I have strong principles in my business and I ensure my team operates by them. I have strong principles for how I operate in other aspects of my life. So why shouldn't I have principles in my relationship and family? I tried it out and it worked. We have four simple principles in our household: kindness, cooperation, respect and love. When someone isn't living up to these principles, we remind them.

What are the principles in your family?

Intimacy & Sex

You are built to have sex and you are built to enjoy it. There is zero shame in wanting sex and a lot of it. Sex is more than an act, it's a way to connect and give and receive energy with your wife. She needs it and so do you to have a healthy marriage. Marriage without sex is equivalent to living with a roommate without benefits.

I'm not a sex therapist, but I do know that some men feel

guilty for wanting sex. You want more of it or you want it in different ways. You may even feel guilty or selfish for wanting it. Even worse, you may be guilted by your wife for wanting it. "All you want is sex!" Have you ever heard that before? Most men have. Don't feel guilty because it's normal to want it. For my podcast, I recently interviewed Dr. John Gray, the author of *Men Are from Mars, Women Are from Venus*. I strongly recommend listening to the interview on episodes 78 and 79 at https://purdeepsangha.com/podcast. Gray shares some great insights on sex.

I've been able to be completely open with my wife about my sexual desires. I've shared all my fantasies with her. I was afraid that she was going to judge me but she didn't. If I'm meeting her needs, she's open to meeting mine. I was surprised by some of her fantasies. She's a pretty timid gal but don't let that fool you. You may be shocked by some of the fantasies that your wife has as well.

Initiating sex can be difficult. Men, just like women, have the need to be desired. You may want your woman to initiate sex because it makes you feel wanted. Tell your wife that you would like her to initiate it more often. Also keep in mind that it's a lot harder for women to get aroused so it's more work for her to get into the mood. If she's not feeling like it, don't hold it against her. You may have to get her into the mood. Don't be afraid to take control. Remember, women like men who take control, and that includes in the bedroom.

Intimacy is a component of sex and you can have intimacy without sex. Intimacy can be shared by holding hands, kissing, hugging, massaging or staring into each other's eyes. Sounds sappy, but try it before you knock it. Men want intimacy just as much as women do. If you're not desiring intimacy with your wife, it's probably because there's a deeper challenge that you have to overcome. I make a point of massaging my wife frequently because it not only relieves her stress but also strengthens that connection between us. Your skin is the largest organ in your body by surface area and it has some of the most sensitive receptor cells. Your skin is the center for pleasure so you might as well take advantage of it.

A healthy relationship has good intimacy and sex. A relationship void of intimacy and sex will eventually wither or die.

Kids

The best thing you can show your kids is that you are madly in love with your wife. For a child, seeing their mom and dad in love creates a safe upbringing for them. It also shows them that having a loving marriage is possible. Most relationships are on the verge of separation or fail completely so the odds of having a successful relationship are already stacked against them. Children learn how to behave in their relationships from their parents. They will copy what you do even if they are consciously trying not to.

There are tons of tainted people out there who have been hurt in relationships who say that amazing relationships only happen in fairy tales. Show your kids that having a loving and beautiful marriage is real.

Set Goals

You and your wife are a team and every team should have goals. Goals create enthusiasm, they create excitement, they create teamwork and they create alignment. 99% of couples don't have mutual goals and they wonder why they have issues. They have goals in every other aspect of life except with each other. If your employees didn't have a mutual target or goal to strive towards, how well would they operate as a team?

You don't need to be military about it and have weekly progress meetings. Goals are meant to be fun. Enjoy it and get your kids involved. It's a beautiful way to bring your family together.

Summary Action Items

1. Take 100% accountability for your relationship.

2. Give your wife what she needs and ask for what you need.

3. Provide value in your relationship.

4. Don't settle.

5. Balance the masculine and feminine energy in your relationship.

6. Avoid resentment.

7. Communicate, communicate, communicate.

8. Have principles for your relationship and family.

9. Have lots of good sex.

10. Set goals and be a good example for your kids.

CHAPTER EIGHT

Fatherhood

"Of all the titles I've been privileged to have, 'Dad' has always been the best."

-Ken Norton

I was driving to one of my retail branches for my weekly rounds when I got a call from my wife. She hesitated for a moment and then explained that she had taken some tests. "I think I'm pregnant."

I remember that moment like it was yesterday. I felt this massive surge of joy run through my body. I couldn't help but break out laughing.

"Why are you laughing?" she asked, "Aren't you scared?"

"No" I replied, "What's to be scared about?"

We weren't planning on getting pregnant. It was a complete accident and just happened. Apparently, he was a Vegas baby based on the timing of conception. We had gone there for a trip and we had a blast. "What happens in Vegas stays in Vegas" but we brought Vegas home with us.

That was the start of a new life for us. I'm a huge animal lover and my friends told me that having my son would feel far deeper than loving animals. I shrugged that off, but when it happened, I realized they were right.

I also heard that having a daughter was even deeper than

having a son. "She'll have you wrapped around her finger." Right again!

When my wife and I got married, my dad sat me down and shared his thoughts with me. We had never had these deep conversations, but now he was serious. He said, "From now on, your biggest responsibility in life is being a good husband and father." Those words have never left my thoughts, and I will share the same words with my son when his time comes.

Your Biggest Responsibility

Imagine being responsible for shaping another life, like sculpting a human being from clay. Your fears, your beliefs, your dreams, your actions, your language, your habits, your happiness and your sadness are transplanted into a beautiful, innocent soul. That's your impact as a father. Your children watch what you do without you knowing. They find meaning in your words that you never knew were there. They mirror your behavior, good or bad. You are their ultimate mentor.

Being a father comes with great joy but also great responsibility. Imagine if all the fathers around the world made raising their children their top priority. The world would be a different place. Instead, fathers spend countless hours at work or play and not enough time shaping their children.

When my son was three, I was rushing through a bedtime story so I could go back to work. I stopped for a moment to reflect. The whole point of me working hard was so I could spend more time with my kids and not have to rush through story time. I was doing things backwards. From that moment on, my morning routine includes giving undivided attention to my son and daughter so they know that my top priority is them.

There are times when you do have to hustle and grind. But there's a boundary where the hustle and grind becomes your whole life, and lots of men have crossed it. The majority of wives I speak to tell me that they would like to spend more time with their husbands, and kids want their dads to be around more often too. A study completed by PEW Research Center in 2017 showed that six out of ten dads felt they spend too little time with their kids and 62% of these men attributed it to having work obligations.

Years later, you may see positive behaviors in your children and be proud, or you may see negative behavior and feel guilt. During my summers as kid, I worked on a family friend's orchard. I started working there when I was nine years old. When I was 15, I just assumed I would be working there the following year but I was wrong. The owner told my dad that he wouldn't be calling me back because he didn't think I had a strong work ethic.

My dad lost it. He didn't even consult with me. He just asked that I have my job back and he would ensure that I worked hard. That's all it took. I worked my ass off that year and the following year they promoted me to foreman. At 16, I was managing other employees and it was the catalyst for where I am today.

Your Role as a Father

You have five main roles as a father: protect, love, provide, teach and be present.

Protecting children goes beyond physical or sexual harm. There's a lot more than sharp objects, scary monsters, and sexual predators that can hurt kids today. There are other factors that endanger your children's ability to live to their full potential. Here are some of them:

- The current school system robs your kids of their imagination. I put my kids in Montessori to protect them from rigid thinking. If you don't have those options, spend time with them at home nurturing their imagination. You'll find that you may have to undo a lot of what is taught in school.

- The media is mostly negative so keep your kids away from it. If you want to share the current events with them, do it in a mindful way.

- Kids have no business on social media unless they're being productive. In-person relationships are far more valuable than online chatter.

- Technology has pros and cons. It's advancing society but we're not paying attention to the long-term impact. Ensure that your kids are using tech to enhance and not replace their intelligence.

- Children are easily influenced and who you introduce to them can matter. Who are the people your kids are looking up to? Every person gives off energy and absorbs energy. When your kids are within a certain vicinity of a person, they absorb their energy. I keep my children away from negative energy people.

Love your children every day and every moment. Love is something you can never give enough of. Even if you're angry at your children, you can love. Even if you need to teach them a lesson for doing something inappropriate, you can love them. You can withdraw other things from their lives but love shouldn't be one of them.

Withdrawing love teaches kids that love in conditional. They learn that they have to do something or please someone in order to be loved. Love your children unconditionally. You may think that they know you love them but the best way to show them is to consistently reinforce it. I kiss and hug my kids all the time. They're still young so they allow me to. I'm getting all the snuggles in right now before they turn them away and I'll have to find other ways to show them that I love them.

Provide your children what they need, not necessarily what they want. Kids need food, shelter, loving parents, growth, exercise, a healthy diet, good relationships, some fun, and a reasonable amount of stimulation. Everything else is a want and wants aren't always good for your kids. Kids getting their wants met but not their needs aren't very healthy.

Teach your kids what they need to know to be happy, healthy and positive contributors to society. It's your responsibility to teach them strong values and principles. This isn't something to outsource to someone else. Showing them the best of your world and allowing them to find the best in theirs is a good approach.

Your family history is another element you can teach your children. I wish I would've learned more of that from my dad. He had so much knowledge and history about India, politics, religion, war and other topics that fascinate me today. After my dad passed away, his younger brother passed away six months later from a heart attack in his sleep. It dawned on me that our entire family history is left with one man, my dad's older brother. I know very little about our history as my dad grew up in India. I've only been back there a few times and only once as a grown man. After my uncle is gone, there's nothing left. Our family history will be non-existent.

Be completely present with your children. Being fully present after a hard day's work can be tough, and kids can sense that. My son will tell me when he thinks I'm not present, and most of the time he's right. Something that helps me with this is making deep eye contact with my kids. Try it, it works.

You Don't Need to Be Perfect

You don't need to be a perfect father to be a good and complete father. You just need to do the best you can. What I most appreciate about my father is that he never pretended to be perfect. He always said. "People are human and they make mistakes. You should forgive them." In a way, I knew he was asking for my forgiveness.

My dad was awesome when he was sober, and not so awesome when he was drunk. When he drank too much, there were times I wished he would just leave us. Occasionally he would drink five days straight, from morning till night. Once he even crashed his truck and spent a few days in jail. He would take his anger for my mom's family out on my mom. It was the oddest feeling to love my dad so much and yet hate him at the same time.

Looking back, I didn't understand what he was going through. He was facing challenges that he didn't know how to get past. Something in his past haunted him. Maybe he never felt loved by his own father, who was in the army for 30 years and was only home two months out of the year. My grandfather did take my dad with him a few times to the army camp, but that was no place to raise a boy either. My brother and I never felt a lack of love from our dad. He was always there for us when we needed him. My dad did the best he could with what he had and what he knew.

Being a good father is a learned skill. You're not born with it. You learn how to parent based on the people around you, including your parents and grandparents. I try to use what was good in my dad and my grandfather, eliminate what was not so good, and learn new skills based on the current information.

I know I make mistakes. I get so focused on work that I ignore my kids at times. But I'm constantly learning and getting better as a dad and that's what's most important.

Don't Be Afraid to Be Tough

Many fathers are allowing their kids to be raised by technology. Others are giving their kids everything they want. Children are becoming entitled, impatient and unappreciative. We're raising a generation of know-it-alls. Today's kids have access to the internet and are way more connected to technology than we were, but that doesn't mean they're smarter. It just means they're always on the internet.

Higher-level thinking in a child's brain doesn't fully develop until they're around 19 years old, so they're not thinking fully logically until then. Meanwhile, they'll look for any weakness you have and exploit it. It's not because they mean any harm. They're just looking for what they want, not what's best for them or what's best for anybody else either.

Your kids will say, "My friend's dad let's her do this." Don't fall for it. You need to be confident and consistent. There are some pretty lazy fathers out there and you don't want to be one of them.

Teach Boys to be Boys and Girls to be Girls

For some people, this is a very sensitive and contentious topic, but not for me. I believe we should be raising our children to understand whether they more strongly relate to being masculine or feminine.

There is nothing wrong with a boy wanting to be a boy, and there is nothing wrong with a girl wanting to be a girl. I also don't find anything morally wrong with a boy wanting to be a girl or a girl wanting to be a boy. But I am very passionate about teaching boys what it means to be masculine and girls to be feminine. Then, it's ultimately their choice what they gravitate toward and are confident with.

Treating boys and girls to be the same is misleading in my opinion. My daughter reacts to things differently than my son, not because of the environment but because she's a girl. My son reacts differently, not because of the environment but because he's a boy. I've tried different approaches throughout their upbringing in order to reveal differences in their natural tendencies. The environment does have an impact, but their biology is even stronger.

I grew up in a household with two boys and my mom taught us to wash dishes and clean the house. Traditionally this was done by the girls in Indian families. One of her favorite sayings was, "God gave you two hands and a brain, so use them." It meant that if you're hungry, make food for yourself. If your room is dirty, clean it up. Do things for yourself even if it's doing things that girls would traditionally do.

We have a lot of females in our extended family and as a child I grew up spending more time with the women than with the men. In our family gatherings, men would sit separately from women. The women would also serve the men first and then eat after. They would also do all the cooking and cleaning. The men pretty much just showed up and had fun. This was an Indian tradition.

Our dad taught us to be men and what went along with being a strong man. Get the job done, be a leader, minimize the noise around you, and the traits associated with the masculine energy. My brother and I grew up around both masculine and feminine energy, and we both gravitate more towards the masculine.

I consider myself lucky to have experienced this upbringing. I learned that gender roles and clear differences between men and women are not wrong or "bad." Clearly defined roles work when people respect each other for who they are and the value they provide.

I teach both my kids to cook, clean, and stand up for themselves. They're in the same extracurricular activities, including piano, soccer, swimming, and karate. I give them equal opportunities, and I also nurture their differences. I play baby with my daughter and foosball with my son because that's their choice.

If you're not going to teach your son to be a man, who will? If you're not going to teach your daughter to be a woman, who will? Society will only give them confusing messages. My brother and I are confident in ourselves because we learned that from our parents, not from society. Take responsibility for raising healthy and confident children but don't force them into something that's not natural for them. Give them exposure to both the masculine and feminine energy and when they're ready, allow them to choose.

Summary Action Items

1. Give your children the attention and time they need.

2. Your main role as a father is to protect, love, provide, teach and be present.

3. Don't try to be perfect. Just be the best dad you can.

4. Don't be afraid to be tough.

5. Teach your boys to be boys and girls to be girls.

PART TWO

The Performance Framework

The Performance Framework is a system that empowers you to consistently perform at your highest potential. You might be a high performer already, but now you can literally double your productivity and impact, or even triple. The Performance Framework will enable you to reach this level without burning yourself out.

The Performance Framework =

Beliefs/Stories + Decision Making

+ Performance Optimization

CHAPTER NINE

Your Beliefs and Stories

"Your beliefs become your thoughts, your thoughts become your words, your words become your actions, your actions become your habits, your habits become your values, your values become your destiny."

-Mahatma Gandhi

For 15 years, Jeff spent most of his waking hours trying to grow his business. The business was passed down to him by his father, who wanted to keep it in the family. Jeff was in his early 50's and lived a modest life. He had been married for over twenty years and had two kids in high school. The business was doing well and always made good money.

Jeff spent his evenings and weekends dealing with issues in the business even though he had a fully capable team to take care of things. Jeff's wife and kids wanted him around more and they were starting to be vocal about it.

I was introduced to Jeff by his investment advisor who was worried about him because he wasn't the healthiest man. He didn't have any known health conditions but he had let himself go. He was very overweight and his advisor was worried that Jeff would never be able to benefit from all the money he was making.

Jeff didn't think he had a problem. He was just doing what his dad had done to build the business. His dad had started the business from scratch all by himself. There were three things working against Jeff at that time. First, he didn't think he had a problem. He believed that working long hours was part of being a business owner. Second, he was doing it alone. Jeff had the belief that he didn't need any help. His dad didn't have a mentor or an advisor, so why would he need one. Third, he believed that a business owner needs to know everything that happens in his business. He had to be hands-on, otherwise the business would fall apart.

Jeff wasn't very keen on working with me. In fact, he thought it was a complete waste of money. His advisor was the one who convinced him that it was in his best interest. I think his advisor even put the bug in his ear that his wife could end up leaving him and take half his net worth if he didn't change.

Jeff came around and we worked on improving his leadership style as well as his lifestyle. It wasn't easy for either of us. It took everything I had to show him that how he was living his life wasn't healthy, and there was no point in having money if he wasn't going to enjoy it. But to Jeff, working was his way of enjoying life. He had little idea of anything else. He had watched how his father lived growing up and believed that's how he should live as well.

Everything changed for Jeff when he realized that his belief system was not his own, it was his dad's. He had total respect for his dad and never thought ill of him in any way. But he wasn't living his own life, he was living his dad's.

When he connected the dots, I saw a look of total sadness on his face. He said, "My dad taught me to be an independent man. This whole time I thought I was being independent, but I was just copying what my dad did." It wasn't long before Jeff was taking vacations with his family and spending more time enjoying his life rather than sitting in his office working.

The best part was that his business grew because he was not around. His staff felt more responsible and accountable for the results and stepped it up. They now had the autonomy to change the way the business operated rather than just go by what he said. It was a win-win situation.

What Are Beliefs?

A belief is just something that is thought to be true. Maybe it is true, or maybe it isn't. Beliefs can be factual like the earth revolves around the sun or imaginary like the Easter Bunny. Factual beliefs can be proven and non-factual can't. You can believe just as strongly in both.

Sometimes you may feel even stronger about non-factual beliefs. I remember going to Bible camp one summer and one of the instructors kept repeating the phrase "jealousy is a journey to hell." He strongly believed in that statement and I started to believe it until I got older and did my research. Jealousy is not the path to hell, it's a natural human tendency that occurs when a person feels inadequate.

Beliefs are things that you understand to be true based on your experiences or even on someone else's. Your beliefs and your identity are highly intertwined. Your identity influences your beliefs and your beliefs influence your identity. You are who you believe you are and who you are determines what you believe.

Remember that a man's identity is the most powerful force in the human mind. Your brain will do everything in its power to remain consistent with that identity. It will even bend how it perceives reality to align with that identity.

You may wonder why some people have crazy beliefs. It's because beliefs are part of who they are based on their identity.

Imagine a tree. Your identity is the roots of the tree and your beliefs are the branches. How those branches grow, the thickness, the health and the rate of growth is highly dependent on the roots. Unhealthy roots lead to unhealthy branches and healthy roots lead to healthier branches.

Why Beliefs Are Important

Aside from your evolutionary drive to survive and procreate, you are belief driven. So if you want to change something in your life, change your beliefs. For example, if you believe that listening to your wife complain about her work will lead to you having more sex, you'll spend more time listening to her. If you don't believe it will help you, you won't.

Most of your beliefs are unconscious and you're not even aware of them. If I asked you to outline your beliefs, you may be able to outline the most obvious ones. But the majority of your beliefs are unknown to you. You have thousands of beliefs and chances are that you wouldn't be able to list a fraction of them. It's not until you make an effort to analyze your beliefs that you can actually identify them.

You can put two men in the exact same situation, with the exact same skills, knowledge, talent and resources and one will come out stronger than the other. It's because of their differences in beliefs. I was around 15 when an older kid challenged me to a shot put competition. He was three years older and was bigger and stronger than I was. At first, I thought I was going to lose. But then something inside of me started to stir up. I felt this unwavering belief that I could beat him. I had such a strong belief that I threw farther than I ever had before and I won. From that moment on, I understood how people could do amazing things just by believing in themselves.

If you're feeling stuck in life or you're not making the progress you want, examine your beliefs closely. Are you frustrated because you believe that you should've been further ahead in life? That belief can cause you to stay in a cycle of self-doubt, so you avoid taking actions that could change your situation.

With every step towards your goals, there is an underlying belief supporting you. With every step in the opposite direction of your goals, there's also an underlying belief slowing you down or stopping you all together.

Strong Beliefs Lead to Strong Results

Men who accomplish amazing things have strong beliefs to back them up.

The stronger the belief, the better the result. Your brain and your body are so interconnected that every cell in your body is connected with every other cell in your body directly or indirectly. Your beliefs go down to your cellular level. When you believe in something with conviction, you can feel your body change. Many scientific studies have shown the positive effects of placebos. Your brain and body can heal just by you believing they can heal.

The only question is, do your beliefs determine your results or do your results determine your beliefs? It's actually a combination of both. The stronger your beliefs, the better your results and the better your results, the stronger your beliefs. So, if you're going to believe in something, do it with everything you have.

Beliefs and Social Groups

Shared beliefs lead to the formation of social groups. People who support the same soccer team usually hang out together to watch the games; people who have the same religious beliefs congregate together; people who have the same political views support each other to a greater degree.

If you and your wife have similar beliefs, you are more likely to have a stronger marriage. If you have strongly opposing beliefs, there's bound to be tension. My wife and I have interesting conversations about formal education. She has multiple degrees and strongly believes in our kids going through the formal education channels. I've attended numerous academic institutions and have numerous designations but I don't believe in the formal education system. I prefer to teach my kids myself and allow them to flourish their creativity. We have to be conscious of belief systems in our marriage or our conversations can easily go down the wrong path.

Associating yourself with people who have different beliefs can be a wonderful experience because it forces you to think differently. I love spending time with people who have differing opinions and beliefs. I get to see the world from a new perspective and I always learn something new. If someone challenges my views, I welcome it.

How Beliefs Are Created

Your beliefs are created by experiences, whether it's reading a book, watching someone else's behavior, or from taking part in an event. The more evidence you have to support the belief, the stronger it gets. However, your brain is a goal-seeking organ and will find whatever you are consciously or unconsciously looking for. You will find evidence to support your existing beliefs whether they empower you or not. Unless it's glaringly evident, your brain will also overlook anything that contradicts your current beliefs.

Most of your beliefs are created unconsciously and many of them are beliefs that have been imposed on you by others. Your upbringing, the education you received, the friends you had in school, the sports teams you joined, and the movies you watched all helped shape the beliefs you have today. Have you ever caught yourself saying something to your kids that your parents said to you? I do it all the time and when I catch myself, I just shake my head.

Because beliefs are highly associated with unconscious memories, you can have a very strong belief and not even remember where it came from. Only seldom do you consciously create a belief, but it does happen. You may experience a life-changing event or have one of those "ah ha" moments. If your car is rear ended by a driver who was texting, you will likely acquire an immediate belief that texting while driving is dangerous. I certainly hope so.

Your Beliefs Create Your Stories

Your life is one big storyline. You are the main character living through a series of chapters of your own story. So are you the victor in your story or the victim? Are you living an empowering story where you live a complete life and get everything you want? Or are you living a story where you have an incomplete life and don't get what you want? The irony is that you are the writer. Only you have the power to create your story.

Based on your beliefs, you create stories in your own head. These stories perpetuate how you think, feel and act. Human beings don't necessarily act based on the facts, they act based on interpretation of the facts. Your brain takes in information – things you see, hear, and feel, things you remember, even things you dream – and then creates what it believes is the most relevant story.

Does your brain make stuff up? All the time. Your brain isn't perfect; its job is to do the best it can with what it has. It's virtually impossible to get all the facts for every situation so it puts together a simulation based on the information it has. It even creates things to fill in the gaps. Were you ever certain that something happened but it never did? It seemed so real to you but others told you that the events were completely different than what you remember. That's just your brain filling in the gaps.

This often happens in marriages. Each spouse's story is completely different even though the facts are the exact same. It's amazing to see how two people who experienced the exact same events can have opposing stories. By focusing more on the facts and less on the story, you'll have a far better relationship.

What happens when you see or read a good story? You get emotionally involved. A good film or book can get people so involved in the story that they feel themselves stepping into it. Special cells in your brain called mirror neurons can trigger the same emotions as the fictional characters in the story. Some anthropologists believe that story-telling was a key evolutionary advantage for the human species. Through stories, we passed on the knowledge and wisdom of previous generations. The stories you replay in your head literally shape your reality. Tell yourself better stories, and your life will be better as well.

Empowering vs Disempowering Beliefs

Are your beliefs making you stronger or weaker? If they aren't empowering you, it's time to change them.

Just like software, your beliefs can be outdated. The beliefs that served you when you were younger may not serve you now. Perhaps you believed that winning at all costs was the best way to play the sport when you were younger. Now you may believe that you play to have fun. I see this quite often with young professionals versus adult leagues. Young men are out there beating each other up on the field while the older guys are out there to socialize and have a beer.

Updating your beliefs and stories will allow you to perform better and keep up with the times. Holding on to old beliefs and stories will slow you down if they aren't relevant. If you believe that the horse and buggy is still the most effective form of transportation, you'll be watching everyone else pass by you. You can still hold on to traditional beliefs as long as they are helping you and not hindering you.

Take a moment to outline the five beliefs that you need right now to perform at your best. Then outline the five stories you need to have to improve your performance. The more you replay these stories in your head, the more your performance will improve. For a quick guide to developing powerful beliefs and stories, go to www.completemanbook.com/resources.

Changing Others' Beliefs

There's no point in arguing with someone about their beliefs. As Dale Carnegie put it, "A man convinced against his will is of the same opinion still." Your job isn't to change people's beliefs, only they can do that. If you have someone in your life that is struggling with their belief system, you should bring it to their attention. Unless you're a professional who does this for a living, it's up to them to change their beliefs.

Summary Action Items

1. Be aware that you have conscious and unconscious beliefs and stories.

2. Be careful who you associate with as you will pick up their beliefs and stories.

3. Go to www.completemanbook.com/resources for a guide to develop powerful beliefs and stories.

4. Don't force others to change their beliefs and stories. You can only influence them.

For additional insight on overcoming self-limiting beliefs go to *The Male Entrepreneur* podcast episode 121 at https://purdeepsangha.com/podcast.

CHAPTER TEN

The Guy Brain

"The human brain is by far the most complex physical object known to us in the entire cosmos."
-Owen Gingerich (Senior Astronomer)

Simon was a kind man who always put others before himself. His wife and sons were his main priorities, and after that it was serving the people in his organization. Simon barely took care of himself. He was overweight, drank and smoked too much.

Simon was a good friend and also a personal mentor who taught me a vast amount in the area of human psychology and motivation. When we first met, I was very much into neuroscience and he pushed me past my comfort zones deep into the realm of emotions.

I worried about Simon's health as I got to know him better. He spent so many years giving to others that he forgot how to do things for himself. He also struggled in his marriage. He stayed married for his kids but he received little in return from his wife. He believed that his natural instincts for sex and intimacy came second to being a good husband and father. But in my opinion, in order to be a good husband and father you need sex and intimacy.

When I explained to Simon the science of how a man's brain and body work, he finally understood. He acknowledged that by subduing his needs, he was hurting himself and his family. He decided to change his approach to his marriage and took control of his sex life. Within days, he seemed like an invigorated man. He wasn't exactly where he needed to be but he made significant progress.

Enjoy It!

It's okay to think, act, and feel like a man. Don't be ashamed of who you are. You should always strive to be a better person but you have natural instincts as a man. If an attractive woman catches your eye while you're walking down the street with your wife, don't feel guilty. You are designed to seek out attractiveness. Respect your wife, but don't beat yourself up because a woman caught your attention.

Understanding how your brain works is important because of widespread misinformation about masculinity as a danger to society. Rarely do people talk about the positives of masculinity. Most front-line workers in dangerous situations such as the police, firefighters, and military are male. It's not because women can't do this work (many do and do it well) but because it requires a high degree of masculine energy.

You are a mix of both nature and nurture. You are the result of your genetics and the environment you were exposed to. The latest studies show that both are equally important. Knowing that your behavior and your desires are influenced by your genes and your environment, you'll be able to live a healthier life.

If you're a naturally outgoing person who enjoys meeting new people, but your wife doesn't want to meet anyone new, you're going to feel trapped. Your environment may be restricting your happiness.

If you're playing basketball with seven-foot giants and you're five foot five, you're going to be frustrated because your genetics don't match up with your environment. Some environments will be better suited to your genetics than others. But never say never. Muggsy Bogues was five foot three and played 14 years in the NBA.

Your brain is unique because it literally controls every other organ in your body. It's also unique because nobody else on this planet has the same brain as you. From the moment you are born, your neurons (brain cells) are developing in unique patterns based on the specific environment to which your brain is exposed. If you were raised in a musical family, the chances are that your brain will adapt better to music than a person who was raised without music. My wife has an amazing ability to play the piano. She can play any tune just by hearing it a few times. She definitely has a genetic gift. The point here is this: your brain is unique based on the genes that your parents passed on to you, plus the environment in which you grew up.

Brain Power

Your brain is constantly changing and evolving. Every time you read a book or learn a new skill, neural connections are forming. For decades it was thought that the brain has a fixed amount of cells, and as a result your intelligence was fixed for life. Science has now shown that this is not the case and that you can increase your intelligence throughout your life.

If you tell yourself that you can't do something, stop right now. Your brain will not do it if you tell it you can't. With enough time and effort, you can program your brain to do whatever you want. The challenge is that most people lack the patience.

You can upgrade your brain's software and computing power with focused effort and this will allow you to move further ahead in life. Working on your brain is about more than just making you smarter. It also includes being able to make more effective decisions, create better habits and manage your emotions. All of these are components needed of The Complete Man.

The Guy/Girl Difference

The brains of males and females are very similar but not identical. Scientists have been able to categorize a brain as either male or female with 93.3% based on 25 unique characteristics.

For the most part, men and women operate in similar fashions. Both males and females have a desire for love, need to be accepted into social groups, to parent and nourish their children. But there are also biological differences that have significant impacts.

Larry Cahill, PhD, a professor of neurobiology, showed that men's brains are larger than women's. But this doesn't result in any difference in intelligence or brain power, as women have more tightly packed cells. A woman's hippocampus, a part of the brain critical to learning and memorization, is also larger. Males have a larger amygdala, which is responsible for emotional processing and recollection.

Researchers from the University of Pennsylvania showed that female brains displayed more coordinated activity between the two brain hemispheres, while male brain activity was more localized. Traditionally, the right hemisphere is associated with emotions and creativity while the left is associated more with analytical processing.

What does this all mean? This research suggests that there are pronounced differences in how men and women behave. These differences go beyond environmental factors. These are ingrained behaviors that are inherent in both sexes. Women have a greater recollection for emotional events than men. Men may have a stronger response to "fight or flight stimuli" meaning if something threatens you, you may have a more intense reaction than a woman would.

Your wife will need to understand that if another man picks a fight with you, you as a man have a greater desire to punch him in the face than she would. Of course, the difference between humans and animals is that we have the controls to think before acting.

Studies of children below the age of 18 months have also demonstrated that boys and girls have different preferences in toys. As much as I try to treat my children the same, it's very clear that my daughter and son have different preferences in toys and activities. They both love to play basketball and air hockey, but my daughter loves dolls and babies. My son couldn't care less and loves throwing things around instead.

Diane Halpern, PhD, past president of the American Psychological Association states that, based on her research, women have better verbal abilities than men and exceed men in reading comprehension and writing ability. Essentially, women are better at communication. She also states that men are better at visualizing two- or three-dimensional shapes. This would suggest that men having stronger skills, for example, in architectural design or playing sports.

Louann Brissenden, M.D., a neuropsychiatrist, research, professor, and former feminism activist, has shifted her views on gender from being a social construct to being influenced by genetics and as well as social factors. She has stated that men are built to explore, to dominate, and to spread their genes, traits that present day society has deemed "negative." Men are also more stern in their parenting style than women.

One of my favorite topics from Dr. Brizzendine's research concerns differences between male and female processing of emotions. Men are not less emotional than women, but they can transition into a problem-solving mindset more easily.

Other studies also show that women are twice as likely to experience depression and men are twice as likely to experience drug or alcohol dependence.

Research doesn't show that men are any better than women. It shows you that you operate on a different software system than females. It also confirms that it's okay to be a guy and to think like a guy. As long as you're not hurting yourself or the people around you, embrace it. If uneasiness about your natural tendencies as a man is holding you back, a deeper understanding of masculinity and the human brain can help you move past that. There's no such thing as being too "manly," once that word is correctly understood.

Goals

Your brain is a goal driven organ. Its main purpose is to move you in the direction that is needed to achieve seven specific goals based on evolutionary development. Studies suggest your brain is driven to:

- Stay away from danger
- Avoid disease
- Develop social affiliation
- Climb a social hierarchy
- Find a mate
- Keep a mate
- Protect your children

These traits are hardwired into your brain based on tens of thousands of years of evolution. The human race has evolved and the context has changed but deep down these seven drivers are still present. If a person with an open cut offers to shake hands with you, you will instinctively hesitate because your brain recognizes the cut as a possible source of disease.

Modern society has added further complexity to these hardwired drivers. Success in your career is associated with social affiliation, hierarchy, and finding a mate. If you don't feel successful, you may fear not fitting in, being ranked at the bottom of your social group, or not being able to attract a suitable woman. Your brain is using out-of-date software to achieve primary goals.

A part of your brain called the Reticular Activating System (RAS) heightens your awareness and intention to align with your goals. If one of your goals is to run a marathon, your RAS will have a heightened sensitivity to topics and stimuli that are associated with marathons. At the same time, it can filter out irrelevant stimuli. Some estimates suggest the brain receives 11 million bits of incoming information per second. It would be highly inefficient for your brain to process all of this information if it wasn't aligned with your goals. Remember that your natural goals also include the seven hard-wired factors mentioned previously.

Your brain is a marvelous tool when used effectively. If you let it run itself, you're in for a challenge. Understanding your brain and setting goals are the first critical steps in achieving greater success and fulfillment.

Happiness

Of all the magical things your brain is capable of, being happy isn't high on the priority list. Unfortunately, your brain isn't designed to make you happy. It's designed to keep you safe and to procreate. That's why men who have the goal of finding happiness never really find it. It's like playing golf. The harder you try to, the worse you get. Being a good golfer is a byproduct of relaxing and following the process. The same applies to your brain and happiness. Aim toward activities, relationships, and goals that make you happy, not toward happiness itself.

Summary Action Items

1. Embrace your male instincts and don't shy away from them.

2. Recognize that you operate on a different software system than females.

3. Determine how the seven evolutionary goals of your brain are impacting your life.

4. Take control of your natural urges instead of them taking control of you.

5. Do things that make you happy rather than aiming directly for happiness.

CHAPTER ELEVEN

How to Make Better Decisions

"You cannot make progress without making decisions."

-Jim Rohn

Early in our marriage, my wife and I went through some tough times. We had completely different backgrounds and upbringings, which really challenged our patience. There were times we just couldn't understand each other. It was strenuous for both of us.

At that time, I was finalizing a number of real estate investments that I started before our relationship began. When the time came to make the most important decisions regarding these investments, I flopped. I was so preoccupied by what was going on between us that I missed a window of opportunity for significant returns. I made a small fraction of what I aimed for in my original plan.

At first, I resented my wife for everything that happened. But when I really thought about it, it had nothing to do with her. It was up to me to make the best decision based on my knowledge, skills, experience and foresight in real estate. She knew nothing about real estate, yet I allowed her overall influence on our life to impact my decisions in this area. I flat out failed to make the best decisions. Not her.

I beat myself up for a while. "How could I be so stupid?" kept going through my mind as well as "I knew better." I consider myself a fairly intelligent person and I usually don't make big mistakes. So, what went wrong? When I analyzed the series of events, the answer was clear. I was in no state to make important decisions. I was stressed, preoccupied and uncertain about our future.

Lack of knowledge or skills were not the issue. It was my decision-making ability. After this realization, I embarked on a mission to understand how to make better decisions.

Better Decisions Lead to Better Outcomes

Life is like a game of chess, a series of cumulative decisions and actions. The better decisions you make, the better outcomes you get. Think of a time when you failed to achieve your objective. Most likely you made ineffective decisions. When you performed at your best, you probably made decisions that led in the right direction.

There are no perfect decisions. If that's what you're aiming for, it's not going to happen. The best approach is to avoid thinking of decisions as right or wrong. Nothing is black or white in reality. There is always some grey. Decision-making is more about making progress in the direction that you want to go. Sometimes you make decisions that cause you to stall or sometimes even side-track you completely. Always ask yourself, "Will making this decision help me reach my goal?"

Commitment

Staying committed is just as important as making a decision. There will be a certain amount of time, effort, and resources needed before you actually see the results. Having planted tens of thousands of apple and cherry trees in my lifetime, I had to accept and appreciate that the trees wouldn't bear fruit for a couple years.

The trees also needed to be painted, sprayed, watered and pruned. All this investment, with no returns at the beginning. Finally, we would see a few apples or cherries here and there. We would even have to remove the fruit in the early years so that the tree would grow faster and healthier. Sometimes the trees would have to be pulled out and replanted. All said and done, the trees didn't fully produce until they were five years old or more. It taught me the meaning of commitment and patience.

Stay committed to your decisions until you truly believe that you've invested enough to see some results. It requires discipline and motivation to get through that initial period of little or no return. If you're trying to lose weight, it's not until you look in the mirror and see the first inch drop off your waistline that you become really motivated. That motivation continues as you see more results.

Your Decision Systems

Your brain is optimized to make both simple and complex decisions. The simple decisions can eventually become unconscious habits, while others require more focused thought. A study done by Dr. Benjamin Libet, a neuroscientist at the University of California, showed that by using an EEG (an instrument measuring electrical impulses in the brain) he could tell one-half second before his subjects made a decision to move their hands that they would make a decision to move their hands with what they thought was "free will." Although you would like to think that you're in conscious control when making decisions, your brain has a system of its own.

Your brain has a natural process for decision-making based on three stages: retrieval, appraisal and response.

First, it retrieves information from the environment using your five senses (sight, taste, touch, smell, and sound) along with proprioception, which is your sense of positioning in space. And there's one other element that most scientists don't speak about. This element is energy, and you have a natural ability to sense it. It's sometimes called the sixth sense, or intuition.

Second, your brain appraises this information based on factors such as your current feelings, your past experiences and memories, and your present knowledge of the situation. This appraisal is passed on to the third stage, which is the response you decide upon.

It's at the point of appraisal and response that you have the greatest power. For example, instead of allowing your brain to make a decision based on what it first brings to the surface, you can ask it to dig a little deeper. If your wife did something to anger you and you initially interpret it as her not caring, ask your brain to think about times that she did care about you. Taking those few extra steps during appraisal could have a significant impact on your response. Ultimately, it's your response that matters. Instead of behaving instinctually and habitually, be conscious and aware of your responses.

Scientists and psychologists have been vastly interested in the topic of the brain and two systems for making decisions. The following system was outlined by Daniel Kahneman, a Nobel Prize-winning psychologist and economist:

System 1, which is considered to be more automatic with very little voluntary control required, can handle making multiple decisions and actions simultaneously. It's like brushing your teeth and showering at the same time.

System 2 concerns complex or important decisions and requires more mental energy and focus. System 2 can only deal with one decision or task at a time, such as deciding to buy a house.

In System 1, your brain is designed to do many simple things at once. It requires little energy. But you may end up creating habits and behaviors that you may not be aware of. You spend a large amount of your day on autopilot. When this happens, you may feel like you're just going through the motions and not making much progress.

System 2 requires more capacity and is designed to help you override System 1 decisions if necessary. If you reach for a bag of chips because that's what you do every evening, it'll most likely be a System 1 decision. If you're on a diet and you reach for a bag of chips, System 2 can approve, reject, or modify System 1's decision. System 2 decision-making can be mentally and emotionally draining. Making complex decisions throughout the day can be exhausting and eventually ineffective.

We are living in a society that is becoming much faster paced. This leads to more System 1, so you may be living on autopilot more than you would like to. To have the life you want, you need to take yourself off of autopilot and take manual control in the areas that need to be adjusted. For the areas that are already working, just keep doing what you're doing.

The 4 R's of Decision-Making

There are a number of factors that influence your decisions, four in particular. Professor Ryan Hamilton of Emory University has broken down decisions making into 4 R's. I've modified the R's based on my experience.

The first R is reference points. You make decisions based on what you already know or information you have access to. If you are driving down the street looking for gas and you see a gas station with a price of $4.00 a gallon and then drive by the next one at $3.25, you're going to pick the second one because the previous gas station had a higher price reference.

The second R is reasons. You do things for reasons that include one or more of the following: avoiding pain, desiring pleasure, not missing out or staying neutral.

The third R is resources. Your brain requires energy and nutrients to operate and the amount of energy you have influences your ability to make effective decisions.

The last R is reduction, which means that your brain will reduce information down to simple terms so that it easily pulls out the most important information and uses that information more effectively. Your brain doesn't like things that are overly complex, so if it has the choice between more detailed information vs. simple information, it will choose simple. That's why the best communicators use shorter sentences and simple words.

Each of the R's has a significant impact on decision-making. Next time you make a decision, write down each of the R's and how you think it impacted your decision. The more you do this exercise, the better you'll get at making decisions.

Indecision

Doing nothing is still making a decision. If you told me that you haven't made a decision yet, I would tell you that you're incorrect. You made the decision to not make a decision – that is, to stay neutral. Men can stay neutral for years and wonder why they never made the money or career progress they wanted. The whole time they fooled themselves into believing they were waiting for the best time to act when in reality they were making a decision to not act. There's a difference.

Unconscious Decisions (aka, habits)

If you're going to be on autopilot, ensure that it's empowering you, not holding you back. I have a regular routine in the morning of waking up, meditating, reading, and working out. These are my morning habits and I don't really think about them. I just do them.

I did have a habit of checking my Facebook ad account all the time because I wanted to know how well our marketing strategy was doing. It was a bad habit to have because, first, Facebook is a waste of time designed to get you hooked and, second, my team was managing the campaign, not me.

Take a tally of everything that you do in a day, from brushing your teeth to tucking your kids into bed. You'll have hundreds of items. This is a very tedious process, but you'll be able to identify many of your habits. Some will be positive, and others you may shake your head at. But the first step in improving your habits is being aware of them. Most men are not!

The Trench

What I call "the trench" is a pit that you dig for yourself after you've made a decision that didn't work in your favor. Instead of changing your course of action, you keep digging into that same trench. Before you know it, you've dug a trench so big you don't know how to get yourself out. I've been there in many aspects of my life from my business to my marriage. Be quick to identify when you've made an ineffective decision, remove your ego and course correct immediately.

Stress

Studies have shown that stress has a negative impact on decision-making. Over time, continuous stress can rewire your brain.

Stress can make you stupid. Some research shows that cortisol, a stress hormone, breaks down hippocampal cells that are responsible for learning and long-term memory. Stress can stunt your learning and memory. If you're constantly stressed, it will hinder your ability to make decisions and achieve the results you want.

If you know someone who is just making one bad decision after another, it could be that they are overly stressed. Cut them some slack. When we had our first child, my wife did some odd things. There were times when I wondered if she had lost her mind. But then I realized that stress was biochemically inhibiting her ability to make good decisions. I kicked myself a few times for getting upset with her and not being as understanding as I could have been.

Social Influence

Your social circle influences your decisions beyond what you think. Your brain is designed to find social affiliation for safety. A natural part of belonging to a social group is looking for their opinion and even approval. Studies have shown that having even one other person in the room while making decisions can have a significant influence on the outcomes. Even people you don't know well can have an impact on your decisions.

Memories and Feelings

Your life experiences shape your future decisions. There is no way around it because your brain has been shaped over the years by your experiences. You have memories and feelings that are ingrained in your brain. These memories and feelings influence your decisions. The question you need to ask yourself is whether you're making the decisions based on how you feel today or how you feel about the situation based on your past.

Confidence Bias

Studies show that having a lot of information may not help you make better decisions. One study took two groups of people, the first was given an average amount of information and the second was given all the information they requested to make the same decision. They found that the second group didn't perform significantly better, but they did have a greater degree of confidence.

Be aware of your confidence bias which is a misleading assessment of your own skills, talents, or intellect. It's great to have confidence but be aware of when it's overstated because it will impact your decisions.

Situational Decision Making

A decision you make today may not be the same decision you make tomorrow. Decision making is highly situational. Some retailers play slower music in their stores to cause buyers to move more slowly so they buy more. Or think of your favorite drink. Is it the same drink you have on vacation? Probably not. On vacation you're in a different environment and you make different decisions. If you had the exact same information, past experiences and if all else was equal, you could still make completely different decisions based on the environment you are in at that time.

Identity

We've said that your self-perceived identity is the most powerful force in your mind. Your identity is one of the biggest influencers in your decision making. You will make decisions consistent with your identity. If part of your identity is being a caring and law-abiding citizen and I offered you a million dollars to shoot an innocent person, you probably wouldn't. That's because you base your decisions on who you believe you are.

Your brain is constantly trying to remain consistent with your identity. Some researchers believe that being consistent with your identity is based on an evolutionary trait. Being part of a social group meant that you would have to be accepted. To be accepted, you would have to be categorized as a specific type of person which meant that you would need to behave consistently. The group would have a difficult time accepting someone who was all over the place and wasn't behaving in a consistent manner.

Your identity can lock you into making decisions in a certain way. Having an empowering identity helps you make better decisions.

Prime State

I never make an important decision after 7:00 p.m. After several years of making key decisions only to regret them later, I realized that I just wasn't making decisions in the right state. I worked hard during the day, which meant that by the evening, I was tired and ready to relax.

After dinner, I was operating at a lower energy level because my brain was trained to relax and chill out. I noticed that when I was in those lower energy states, I would be a little more fearful and hesitant. I was even questioning my own confidence and my ability to be a leader and entrepreneur. I wasn't conscious that this was happening. I would still answer a few emails here and there and make some important decisions which were not effective.

I realized that because I was in a lower energy state in the evening, I wasn't using System 2 thinking. Instead, I was acting habitually, which is not effective for running a business. I was in survival mode.

As mentioned previously, your brain consumes more energy in System 2. System 1 is very much about survival. You want to be in a high energy state anytime you make important decisions. You don't want to make decisions when you're stressed or in a low energy state. Hold off on your decisions until you're more energized.

Take One Action Step

As soon as you make a decision, take at least one step in your chosen direction. If you decide today that you need to go on vacation, book your time off now. Or if you've decided to lose weight, call a personal trainer now.

When my clients make a decision, I force them to take one step towards the decision immediately. I will not let them go until they do because I know it's the most crucial step. The first step is the most important to create the momentum you need to keep moving forward.

Reflection

Becoming a master of decision making requires you to constantly reflect on your decisions and actions. The best chess players go back and replay the game they played to find their best and worst moves. The more you reflect, the better you get. Reflection allows you to capture the elements that allowed you to make great decisions. Reflecting will also cause you to see the elements that led you to making decisions that held you back.

Summary Action Items

1. To download a quick guide on the steps to making better decisions, go to

   www.completemanbook.com/resources

2. Be committed to your decisions.

3. Course correct quickly when you make a decision that doesn't work for you.

4. Watch out for being too confident with your decisions.

5. Identify your empowering habits vs. disempowering habits.

6. Avoid consistent stress.

7. Be in a prime state when making decisions.

8. Always take one step in the direction of your decision immediately after making it.

9. Reflect, reflect, reflect on your decisions.

CHAPTER TWELVE

Performance Optimization

"An ounce of performance is worth pounds of promises."

-Mae West

"Purdeep, you're done already? How did you get done so fast?"

I've heard this from many people throughout my life. Not from my parents, of course, because they were the hardest working people I knew. For them, I didn't get things done fast enough.

They were immigrants who built everything they had from scratch. With little education and no technical skills, they only knew how to work hard. Beyond that, they also had to learn how to work smart. They made minimum wage for many years before they purchased their own orchard and ran their own business.

They learned to be smart and efficient with every resource they had, and they developed systems to get more done with less effort. They were all about leveraging every resource they had.

Waste was not an option because that meant not being able to provide for the family. My dad was also sending money back to his parents and brothers in India so they could live a better life as well. I'm not sure how my parents did it but I'm proud to be their son. I give my mom extra credit since she never once complained that my dad was sending money back to his family in

India while he had kids to feed here. She was an understanding and supportive woman.

Because of my parents, I grew up working hard and smart. I had my first official job at nine years old making boxes at a cherry packing facility. As I got older, I worked all summer, and on weekends during the spring and fall. While my friends would be going on summer vacations with their families or going to camp, I worked 10-hour days six days a week. During the busy season, I would wake up at 4:00 am and work 12-14 hour days, including Sundays. The only off days were the odd Sunday and the days it would rain.

My wife thinks this was child labor, and it felt like it. But looking back, it was the best experience of my life. I learned how to work hard and get the job done. No excuses. I've built on the same principles over the years to develop a system that allows me to optimize my performance and get the results I want in all aspects of my life.

Talking gets you nowhere. Only action and performance will get you where you want to go.

Motivation

Motivation is fuel for performance. With it, you have a supercharged engine. Without it, your engine is stalled. Motivation can be expressed as a simple equation:

$$\text{Motivation} = \text{Desire} \times \text{Progress} \times \text{Purpose}$$

Desire is the degree to which you want something. Is it just a nice thing to have, or is it something you can't live without? The intensity of both your desire and your progress has a multiplying effect on your overall motivation. Progress means moving in the direction of what you're trying to achieve. Progress needs to be made even if it's not quite the progress you want. Sometimes you may have to look hard to find it. The key is how you feel about your progress, not the progress itself. For one man, making an extra $100k may feel amazing but to someone else, it could seem insignificant.

Purpose is the underlying reason for doing what you're doing. What is it that you really want? Is it more love, more confidence, more challenge, more passion or more fulfillment? Whatever the reason, it must be good enough to move you. The stronger your reason, the greater your motivation.

Research shows that, for most people, purpose falls into one or more of six categories. The first is finding status with peers. The second is finding status with experts or authorities. The third is the need for acquisition, which could mean gaining a new skill or buying a house. The fourth is achieving independence and showing others that you are self-sufficient. The fifth is the desire to defeat competition. The sixth is the desire for excellence as an end in itself.

Productivity

One of my early mentors mentioned that demand equals productivity. The moment I heard this, it made total sense. The more demand you put on yourself within a specific time frame, the more productive you will be.

A study by John Pencavel, a professor of economics at Stanford University, showed that productivity of employees declined sharply after working 50 hours per week. Employees working 70 hours a week accomplished the same amount of work as those working only 55 hours. Working more doesn't equate to getting more done so stop fooling yourself. Just because you work late or on weekends doesn't mean you're progressing. It just means you are putting in more time.

The best way to be highly productive is by putting a high demand on yourself and being laser-focused at the same time. Distractions kill productivity at work and at home. As much as I'm in favor of an open-door policy at work, I believe it should be for only certain times during the day. Otherwise it's easy to get distracted and that's how your productivity drops.

I had a friend ask me to help him build his tool shed. I put my head down and worked while he kept chatting away. He said, "Man, why don't you just chill? We can have a few beers while we're doing it."

I turned to him and said, "It'll take us three hours to do this if we focus on getting it done and then we can spend five hours chilling out and having beers. Or would you rather spend eight hours sweating in the sun with no time to relax later?" He got the point and got back to work.

The Zone

Have you ever experienced a moment when you had a clear goal in your mind, you lost all sense of time, you were on the top of your game, you were laser focused, there were zero distractions in your mind, you were getting things done, and you felt you were in total control regardless of what came your way? It was almost like an outer-body experience.

I call that "the zone," as do many athletes. It's also called a "flow state." If you haven't experienced this before, it may sound strange at first. But if you speak to an athlete who has played an intense sport like boxing or even played in an intense situation like a playoff game, you will find that this experience is fairly common. I attribute my ability to outcompete my competitors and achieve what I have to being in the zone more often than not.

The zone is where you want to operate consistently. It's a state where you get more done with less effort, in less time. Instead of feeling stressed, it feels natural. There may even be a sense of relaxation even though your mind and body are in a state of high demand and productivity.

I think of the zone as an opening to a different dimension. There's only a small window of opportunity to get in, but once you're in, the possibilities are endless. For more information on how to get into the zone, go to: www.completemanbook.com/resources.

Characteristics of Optimal Performers

Would you be able to tell just by looking at someone if they were an optimal performer? Maybe or maybe not. Performance psychology studies have outlined a number of characteristics that optimal performers have including: they are intrinsically motivated rather than extrinsically; they have strong dedication to their goal; they take things one step at a time so they don't get overwhelmed; they prioritize and focus on attaining their goal; they give it 100%; they are self-reliant and don't let others hold them back.

I've seen certain shared characteristics in men who achieve completeness in their performance. They have a burning desire for their goal and strong belief that they'll attain it. Their belief is so strong that it becomes a certainty, so they remain positive and optimistic throughout the journey.

Become a Master

If you're going to aim for a goal, become a master along the way. Dabbling in something, whether it's a new business venture or a relationship, only gives you average to poor results. Entrepreneurs who have multiple startups face this challenge. They dabble in numerous ventures hoping that one of them will be their golden ticket. They have better chances focusing on one or two instead.

A pet peeve of mine is men bragging about reading one book a week. Wow, you read one book a week but how much of that book did you master? Success doesn't come from gathering knowledge, it comes from mastering knowledge.

Mastery is what you should be aiming for just as much as the goal itself. The best basketball players become masters of their game because they know mastery leads to victory. The best surgeons master their operating skills because that's what's going to give them the reputation of being the best. If you want an awesome marriage, master the skill of being the best husband. If you want to raise awesome kids, master the art of being a father.

Here are some principles for becoming a master:

- **Practice with precision** – Poor practice leads to poor results. Practice with clear intent and intensity.
- **Be consistent** – Mastery comes with consistency and there is no short-cut.
- **Be deliberate** – Know what you want and be intentional about it.
- **Seek feedback** – Determine what's not working and correct it immediately.
- **Find a mentor** – All masters had a mentor.
- **Create a challenge** – Constantly challenge yourself enough to keep it interesting but not too much so you get discouraged.
- **Try new approaches** – Mastery is about learning and growth. Find new ways of doing things.
- **Celebrate your milestones** – If you've made progress, congratulate yourself for it.

- **Have will power** – Hang in there. Even when you think you're done, keep going. Never give up!
- **Think easy** – If you think it's hard, it's going to be hard. If you think it's easy, it's going to be easier.
- **Turn uncomfortable into comfortable** – Learn how to turn things you don't enjoy into things that you do enjoy.
- **Master the small things** – When you master the small things, you can master the big things. And you can't master the big things until you can master the small things.

Keeping Track and Measuring

Do you track and measure your performance? If you're like most guys, you'll say, "Yes, I do."

But if I asked you to show me the results on paper, would you be able to do that? Probably not. Men like to keep track of things in their heads, but this tracking can be easily manipulated. You'll create scenarios or excuses to justify a lack in progress.

If your goal is to lose 20 pounds in four months, then you should on average lose five pounds a month. If after two months you haven't lost 10 pounds, you'll tell yourself that you still have two months to go and you'll make up for it somehow. It's a better idea to break it down to a weekly goal of 1.25 pounds per week. That way you don't have to wait a whole month before you find out that you're not on track.

Set key performance indicators (KPI's) to which you must hold yourself accountable. That can be tough to do, but it's the most important thing you can do. If you have difficulty holding yourself accountable, find someone you respect to hold you accountable.

I was shocked when I discovered that men would pay me just to hold them accountable. For me it made no sense, because I held myself accountable for almost everything I did since I was a kid. But not everyone was raised by a military grandfather and two driven parents who I worked with side-by-side until I was an adult.

If you're not tracking on paper, you're not tracking it at all. Set your KPI's, write them down on paper and hold yourself accountable.

Keep it Clean

Clutter on your desk, in your office and at home, takes up mental capacity and distracts your train of thought. If you pride yourself on the numbers of folders on your desk, it's time to file them away. It's hindering your performance.

Uncompleted tasks can also take up mental capacity. That's why you can be sitting with your family and still thinking about that one thing you forgot to do at work even though you know you can't do anything about it at that moment.

Do a regular clean-up of your work and living space as well as your outstanding tasks. It'll help you stay focused and improve your performance. It feels good too.

The Wall

You've heard of "the wall." It's the point that athletes face when their body tells them "no more, I'm done." But they still go on to complete the race and win. That's because the mind is more powerful than you imagine and your body will obey your mind.

The best feeling is on the other side of the wall, when you've pushed through. It's a feeling of pure power and even ecstasy. Athletes, like decathletes, speak about getting past the wall and feeling as though they had left their bodies.

My trainer, Billy Beck, trained The Rock for seven years so he knows how to push people. His workouts are grueling and I hit the wall many times. But once I'm through the wall, I feel a physical sensation of electricity flowing through my body. I feel like someone just plugged me into an electrical socket. The only way to describe it is with one word: powerful. To listen to a powerful interview with Billy Beck on *The Male Entrepreneur* Podcast, go to episode 63 at https://purdeepsangha.com/podcast.

To get through the wall, do these three things: focus on your goal or outcome, live in the identity you create to reach that goal, and focus on the process rather than the outcome. There is one additional step you can take and that is tell yourself a third-person narrative. This has been shown to increase performance. You could picture someone telling a positive story about your accomplishments or maybe even a news broadcast. It may seem egotistical at first but it works.

Rest

Your mind and body need rest. Continuing to work hard without recovery only does harm in the long-term. Not resting will catch up with you. It always does.

Some guys think that working like a dog is a status symbol. The guy who works the most hours is at the top of the food chain. That's absurd, because the guys who can perform for years are the ones who work hard but also rest along the way. Short-term gain can create long-term pain.

Momentum

Momentum is a powerful force. You either have it or you don't. There is no in-between. Once you have the momentum, you are like a freight train. Almost nothing can stop you unless you choose to stop yourself. All it takes is a few consecutive wins to create momentum.

External circumstances can easily distract you if you allow them to. Keep your eye on your goal and keep the momentum going even if it's at a slower pace. Don't stop the train.

Slow Down to Speed Up

There are times that you have to slow down a little, or maybe even a lot, to speed up your overall progress. Perhaps you're overlooking key facts or you're letting things fall through the cracks. Or maybe you're so focused on the results, that you're not mastering the process along the way. Taking a moment to step back, reevaluate and adjust your approach is needed at times. It's better to do it yourself and be in control than have it forced upon you.

Prioritize

Rather than trying to do everything at once, make a list, prioritize it, and do each of those things well. There is no shame in saying "now is not the right time" or "I'll do that later." A novice wastes resources and energy doing things he shouldn't be doing. A master knows where to allocate his resources to get the highest return for his efforts.

Weaknesses

"Focus on your strengths and not your weaknesses." That is the silliest idea I've ever heard.

If you're a CEO and you don't know enough about financials to ask relevant questions, you can't run the ship as well as you think. So, you've got to develop at least a working knowledge of financials.

There are just certain skills and abilities that you absolutely need in order to be successful. So focus on your strengths, but also strengthen your weaknesses.

Channel Fear

Fear, like all emotions, is a form of energy. You can let it control you and take you over or you can take control of it and channel it in the right direction. Use it to your advantage. The best way to channel fear is to be aware of when it's present and avoid downplaying it.

Fear can linger unconsciously for long periods of time without your conscious awareness. Bring it to the surface early on and then focus on projecting that fear as anticipation or excitement. Fear and excitement are similar in feeling but accompanied by differing thoughts.

That's why when you were younger, you did things you wouldn't imagine doing now. Back then, fear would lead to excitement. Now fear is just fear. Be a kid again.

Optimal Stress

An optimal stress level creates better performance. Not having enough stress might not get you going and too much might cripple you. Stress has two variables, intensity and duration:

$$Stress = Intensity \times Duration$$

An optimal stress level requires a correct proportion of intensity and time. Perhaps it's a low, medium or even high degree of intensity. Pair that with a short, medium or longer time duration. What's optimal for you might not be optimal for someone else.

Be cautious as a prolonged stress duration can have harmful effects on your body and mind. Always take a break when needed.

Reasons for Not Performing

Every guy has reasons for not performing and there are typically many. The trick is to reduce your reasons for not performing by consolidating them. Maybe you're looking to start a new business but you don't have the time to do it, and you can't afford it right now. Consolidate them into a single reason: perhaps the timing isn't ideal.

On the other hand, you can also split one reason for doing something into many reasons. You're looking to start a business because the market needs the product you're going to sell. You can break this down into: consumers will easily pay because there's a massive demand; if you don't do it now, someone else will; and you have another kid coming so you need the money. One reason became three.

Don't let your reasons control you. Control your reasons.

Waste

We live in a very wasteful society and it hinders your performance. The more intentional you are about using the resources you have like your time, money and energy, the better your performance will be.

Business operations is one of my key expertise. Over the years, I've studied and consulted for corporations on how to become more intentional about their resources so they waste less and achieve more. I even received my blackbelt in lean operations which is not a martial arts degree. It's a discipline to streamline operations, remove waste and make systems more efficient.

I spent time in Japan learning from Honda, Toyota, and Nissan, which are all masters of lean operations. What astonished me beyond the business operations was the culture in Japan. They don't waste anything. The trains leave exactly on time, there are hardly any garbage cans and in the major cities, the commuters use bikes. The Japanese culture is all about performance. Much of this has to do with their ability to remove waste and maximize their resources.

Summary Action Items

1. Keep your motivation strong with intense desire, progress and purpose.

2. Keep your productivity high with high demand and focus.

3. Go to www.completemanbook.com/resources to download the formula for getting into "The Zone."

4. Become a master, not an amateur.

5. Track and measure your progress.

6. Keep your mind and environment clean.

7. Keep going and don't stop at "the wall."

8. Rest when you need to.

9. Keep the momentum going.

10. Slow down to speed up.

11. Prioritize!

12. Work on your weaknesses.

13. Channel your fear and use it as a form of energy.

14. Find your optimal stress level by testing out the intensity and time duration.

15. Consolidate your reasons against and multiply your reason for achieving what you want to achieve.

16. Maximize your resource allocation and waste very little.

CHAPTER THIRTEEN

Vitality

"Live a vital life. If you live well, you will earn well. If you live well, it will show in your face; it will show in the texture of your voice. There will be something unique and magical about you if you live well. It will infuse not only your personal life but also your business life. And it will give you a vitality nothing else can give."

-Jim Rohn

I looked over at Gerard and he was dripping with sweat. I could not believe how drenched he was. We had only been walking ten minutes to catch a cab but he looked like he'd been walking for days. I thought he was going to have a heart attack and I'd be the lucky guy to perform CPR on him. I've never had to perform it but I was ready.

Gerard was in his mid-forties but he looked ten years older. He smoked and drank when he was under pressure, which was pretty much every day. He was a high-powered executive and the go-to guy. Everyone went to him with their problems and he spent more time helping others than helping himself. He had an amazing heart and would do anything for anyone. He was just one of those genuine guys that you could count on. But Gerard's poor health was taking a toll, and he was close to 90 pounds overweight.

I was growing fond of Gerard. Most men are one dimensional, but Gerard had many layers. He was a brilliant strategist and a master of communication. I learned from him and he learned from me. It was a win-win relationship.

Gerard was a perfect candidate for a stroke or heart attack. He was overweight, smoked, drank, and was under constant stress. He also had a family and I knew they too were worried about him.

I slowly convinced Gerard to exercise regularly and reduce his smoking and alcohol. I even went to the gym with him to get him started. I had been a personal trainer from the age of seventeen until my early twenties so I knew how to get him going.

Gradually Gerard got into the habit of exercising and even hired a personal trainer. He reduced his drinking and smoking by half. He didn't have any intentions of quitting smoking or drinking all together but at least he was doing something to improve his vitality.

In a short time, he lost a few inches off his waist. That gave him a huge boost in confidence because he hated his gut. As he began to make lifestyle changes, you could see the life flow back into Gerard. Rather than looking like a chain smoker and a drinker, he looked like a vibrant man.

Vitality is Life

Vitality is the health of your inner world. The stronger, healthier and more balanced you are internally, the deeper you experience the external world. Money and a big house mean nothing if you don't have the vitality to fully experience them.

Vitality fuels persistence toward completeness. A man who lacks vitality will eventually give up, not because he doesn't want victory but because he doesn't have the energy to achieve it. What would your life be like if you had double or triple the vitality?

You are energy, pure and simple. Every cell in your body consumes energy and expels energy. The more energy you have in your system, the better the system functions. This energy is vitality.

How do you generate more vitality? Because you are a spiritual being with a physical body, you must take care of both. Four intertwined components are essential for developing boundless vitality: mind, body, emotions, and spirit. When one grows, so will others. When one is starved, others will starve as well. Exercising and nurturing all four are required to maximize your level of vitality. Men tend to nurture physical and mental elements and allow emotion and spirit to go without much attention.

Taking care of your mental, physical, emotional and spiritual growth isn't rocket science. Yet men neglect certain elements because they're preoccupied with goals of achievement and success. But investing in yourself is the best way to make progress toward a goal. After all, no one can get you there except yourself.

The first thing I take care of in the morning is me. I train and feed myself first because I know that when I take care of myself, I perform at my best. The stronger I am mentally, physically, emotionally and spiritually, the better I can serve my family, my business, and the men I work with.

Mental Vitality

Your mind needs exercise for a number of reasons. First, the world is changing rapidly. What you know today may not help you tomorrow, so keeping your mental skills finely tuned is critical for business and personal success. Skills like problem solving, creative thinking, memorization, intuition, learning, reading, and writing.

If you don't exercise your brain, it deteriorates over time. That doesn't mean that older people are slow. It just means that your cognitive functioning declines with age. Exercising both your brain and your body has been shown to slow down the degenerative effects.

From a spiritual perspective, your brain is an antenna connected with universal genius. The sixth and seventh chakras are located in the brain. The sixth chakra is associated with intuition, ideas and guidance and the seventh is associated with a higher consciousness. By tapping into both, you can engage creative genius. But this requires intentional effort and practice.

Here are some best practices for your mental vitality:
- Eat healthy
- Exercise
- Read
- Practice writing
- Learn new skills
- Sleep well
- Meditate
- Practice mindfulness techniques
- Avoid too much sugar or alcohol
- Avoid drugs
- Go for walks in nature
- Reduce your stress
- Avoid negativity
- Take naps
- Practice optimism
- Engage in thoughtful conversations

Physical Vitality

Your body is your vessel. If the ship is sturdy and in top shape, it weathers the storms and cruises to its destinations. If it's full of holes, it must stop to get patched up or eventually it sinks.

Be conscious and in tune with your body and don't ignore it. It's designed to tell you when it needs something. If your body is telling you that it needs rest, give it a rest. If your body is craving sex, give it sex. Overindulgence isn't good either, of course. That's why you have a brain: to override any unhealthy cravings of your body. There's a fine line between healthy and unhealthy desires that you must learn to identify.

Here are some best practices for your physical vitality:
- Healthy diet
- Exercise
- Deep breathing
- Meditation
- Practice mindfulness techniques
- Take cold showers
- Massages
- Daily walks
- Avoid too much sugar or alcohol
- Avoid drugs
- Reduce your stress
- Avoid negativity
- Sleep well
- Receive energy healing

I recommend only what I've used or have seen others use for proven benefit. My wife and I have recently been experimenting with red light and near-infrared therapy. We've been using it to heal tissue, injuries, and rejuvenate our muscles. It seems to be working very well so I encourage you to look into this.

Emotional Vitality

Do things that you enjoy. I can't make it any simpler. Have hobbies that you enjoy doing. Hang around with people you enjoy hanging around with. Have relationships with people who make you laugh. Make yourself laugh. Studies show that you'll live a happier and longer life if you have quality relationships.

If I'm on the phone with my mom and she starts a negative conversation that I've heard from her before, I end the call quickly. My wife tells me I'm being rude but there's a reason for it. I do it for her emotional health. If she needs to vent, I'll listen once for sure and maybe twice but no more than that. If she needs help, I'm here to help. If she wants someone to join in on her negativity, no thanks. By allowing her to indulge in her negativity, I'm hurting her rather than helping her. When people have consistent pity parties, it hurts everyone emotionally.

Here are some best practices for your emotional vitality:
- Healthy diet
- Exercise
- Deep breathing
- Meditation
- Practice mindfulness techniques
- Daily walks
- Avoid too much sugar or alcohol
- Avoid drugs
- Reduce your stress
- Avoid negativity
- Sleep well
- Laugh
- Have sex
- Have loving relationships
- Express your feelings
- Receive energy healing

Spiritual Vitality

Your spiritual energy is your soul's direct connection to the source energy of the universe, which is infinite because the universe itself is infinite. In fact, the universe is continuously expanding.

Spiritual vitality is the most important energy to nurture because it feeds all your other vitalities. A healthy spiritual energy leads to a healthy mind, a healthy emotional state, and a healthy physical body.

Spiritual vitality is an energy that you may not directly feel at first. Over time, you can develop the highly focused states of mind that are compatible with meditation or a mindfulness practice. But you can also tap into spiritual energy by other means such as daydreaming, art, and tantric sex.

Ancient Indian health traditions describe spiritual energy using a system of levels called chakras. This is based on the premise that there are energy focal points throughout your body. Each focal point represents and projects different frequencies of energy which correspond to different aspects of life.

The term "chakra" means wheel in Sanskrit. Each chakra is continuously revolving like a wheel. Each chakra works together with other chakras to form unified frequencies that are uniquely yours. No other being has the same frequencies as you, yet your frequencies connect with all other frequencies to create a unified consciousness.

The chakras correspond to different areas of your body, which in turn correspond to an organ or gland that is critical to your physical health.

Here is a brief outline of each chakra:

- **Root Chakra** – Located in the base of the spine and associated with your kidneys and skeletal system. It's connected to your adrenal glands. The root chakra grounds you to nature and your basic need for security and stability. It's your energy center for keeping your life vibrant and sustainable.

- **Sacral Chakra** – Located in your testes and ovaries for women. The sacral chakra is associated with your body's desires for food, sex and pleasure. It's connected to your motion and emotions as well. It's your energy center for your physical health and well-being.
- **Solar Plexus Chakra** – Located below your sternum and connected to your pancreas. It's associated with your gut instinct and personal power. It's your energy center for your personal identity.
- **Heart Chakra** – Located in the middle of your chest and connected to your thymus gland. It's associated with love, peace and joy. It's your energy center for love and life.
- **Throat Chakra** – Located in and around your throat and connected with your thyroid gland. It's associated with communication. It's your energy center for self-expression.
- **Brow Chakra** – Located between your eyes and connected with your pituitary gland. It's associated with mental applications and creativity. It's the energy center for the power of your mind and wisdom. Some practices refer to the brow chakra being connected to the pineal gland and the crown chakra being connected to the pituitary gland.
- **Crown Chakra** – Located at the top of your skull and connected with your pineal gland. It's associated with divinity. It's the energy center for connecting with a higher consciousness.
- **Soul Chakra** – Located about eight inches above your head and connected with your aura. It's the collectiveness of all chakras. It's the energy center for spiritual selflessness.

Here are some best practices for your spiritual vitality:
- Meditation
- Mindfulness techniques
- Yoga
- Tantric sex
- Spend time in nature
- Receive spiritual healing
- Give spiritual healing
- Live with joy
- Show love and kindness to all beings

Summary Action Items

1. Take care of yourself first.

2. Nurture all four areas of vitality: mental, physical, emotional and spiritual

3. Follow the best practices in this chapter.

CHAPTER FOURTEEN

The Complete Businessman

"The most important asset you have as a businessman is you."

-Purdeep Sangha

Wes and I got to know each other through a conference we both attended. He was a very successful CEO and we both had a passion for business strategies. After a few conversations, he asked if he could put me on a retainer to help him through some major changes he was making in his company.

I told him how much I charged and he said that he didn't have the budget at the time. A few days later he called me back and told me that he reprioritized his budget for us to work together.

Our first three strategy sessions were focused strictly on business and we worked through some significant challenges Wes was facing. The fourth session was slightly different, as the conversation turned toward his skills as a CEO.

Wes was somewhat reluctant to talk about his communication style or other aspects of his leadership. He was obviously a skilled executive or he wouldn't have been CEO of such a big enterprise. I didn't want to put him on the defensive so I didn't really pursue talking about his personal style as an executive or related issue. After all, he was paying me for business strategy consultations, not personal growth opportunities.

Wes caught me by surprise in our fifth session. He was at least 15 to 20 years older than me and ran a massive company so I'm sure he felt some awkwardness when he said, "Purdeep, I know I'm good at what I do, but I also know that I can do better. Or rather, I can be better."

I gave him credit. It's not easy for an accomplished man to admit to someone much younger that he has work to do on himself. But Wes was smart. He knew that the more he became complete as a man, the better his business would operate.

You Are Your Most Important Asset

You are a complex system of thoughts, emotions, energy, processes, strategies and tactics. Similar to other complex organizations, you need a CEO to run your organization. You first need to be the CEO of yourself. The better you are at running yourself, the more effective you will be in the other roles you have in your life as a husband, father, and businessman.

CEO's get paid the big bucks because they know how to captain a ship. A ship without a captain is just a hunk of material in the water. But a ship with a master captain can be many things. It can be a vehicle for wealth, connection, exploration, and all sorts of experiences. By developing your internal skills, you become a bigger asset to yourself and those around you. You multiply your ability to attain wealth, success, and completeness.

Invest in Yourself

As a professional business strategist, I can easily give you strategies for business growth and improvement. But awareness of how you operate and who you are internally is a larger objective. In other words, the foundation of being a complete businessman is becoming a Complete Man.

First, invest in yourself. The more time, energy and resources you invest in yourself, the more your business or career will advance. Regarding this, there is a stark difference between Americans and Canadians. American businessmen are much more open to investing in an advisor, consultant, or personal coach. I'm sure there are some deep cultural reasons for this that could fill a book by themselves.

Who performs better? The guy who invests $50k in himself or the guy who spends $50k on his business. By far, it's the guy who invests in himself. Your business is an expression and an extension of you. Your external world is a direct reflection of your internal world. If you had the skills, knowledge, tools, systems, and wisdom internally to get what you want, you'd already have it. If you don't have what you want, it's because you're not at the level you need to be internally. Therefore, investing in yourself is critical.

Why Are You Doing What You're Doing?

Why are you in the business you're in? Why do you have the career that you have? You may spend at least half of your waking hours working in your profession, but for what? These are simple questions but they can be difficult to answer.

Your work should provide one more of these elements: income for the lifestyle you want; pride in what you do; and enjoyment from doing it. If your work doesn't give you any of these, you should rethink your work. If your work gives you all three, congratulations!

Ideally, a profession that gives you all three will keep you motivated for a long time. When you lose motivation, you lose "mojo," as Austin Powers put it. The more mojo you have, the better your results – and the better your results, the more mojo you get. It's a cycle.

Which of the three elements is most important? It really depends on you. What keeps you motivated? I know from coaching successful men that money only motivates them until they get bored. Eventually they lose interest and move on to something that presents a challenge, creates an impact, or brings enjoyment.

You can have all three elements and don't let anyone tell you otherwise. Right now, your career may not provide you all three, but it can eventually. The key is not to settle. When your gut tells you that something is missing in your profession, it's time to make a change. And it's never too late. I've worked with men in their 60's who have shifted their professions and have done very well. Believe it or not, the opportunities really are endless.

You Are Marketing Yourself

As a businessman, you are constantly marketing yourself so you need to be great at it. You are in the business of influence. Your job is always to influence people to work with you to achieve a business goal. If you can't market yourself, people will not have faith in your leadership and they will not see a reason to work with or for you.

Your most important operational skills as a businessman are influence and communication. Your communication should impart energy as well as information. Energy is what influences people to move, and act. To upgrade your communication and influence skills, go to www.completemanbook.com/resources.

Authority

Authority is an expression of power and it often has negative connotations. Unchecked authority is obviously a detriment and can be abused. But we also depend on individuals with legitimate authority. You go to a medical specialist because they have the authority to help you with your condition. You call the police when there is a crime because they are the authorities to help you in that situation. If you were getting robbed, you probably would not call your cousin Bob who owns three shotguns, five rifles, two rocket launchers and a machete. You'd call the cops.

You want to be known as an authority in your work. No one wants to deal with the average man. If you and your wife are looking to buy a new home and your neighbor says, "Hey, I know a guy who can help you find a home" or, "Hey, I know the go-to guy for helping couples find new homes," which one would catch your attention?

Create your niche and own it. There's nothing wrong with being a jack of all trades, and I actually pride myself on being an authority in different areas of business and personal performance. But I focus on working with businessmen who want to experience complete victory. Also, I do not work with men who are solely focused on having a one-dimensional life. I work with men who are family-oriented or who aspire to be family-oriented. After years of focused effort, training, growth, experience and innovation, I'm known as an authority for helping family-oriented businessmen have it all.

Being the authority allows you to benefit outside of business as well. Some of the best personal relationships I've developed over the years stemmed from my business relationships. These connections and relationships have broadened my horizons in other areas such as health, relationships, travel, history, and even spirituality. Being the complete businessman will improve your quality of life overall.

Systems Sell

Knowledge is useful but not as valuable as systems. If people can use your knowledge, it's often on a one-off basis. What they can consistently use, and what they really need, is a system.

Let's use a personal trainer as an example. A personal trainer can be knowledgeable about fitness and health and still not be able to get their clients results. Why? Because they haven't converted that knowledge into a usable system that their client can execute. Systems allow you to get repeatable results and systems can be continuously improved and fine-tuned over time.

It doesn't matter how much you know until you can actually transfer that knowledge into a system that can help yourself or others. When you do this, two things happen. First, you go from being knowledgeable to being an asset. Assets generate wealth; knowledge is just "good to have." Second, you can scale your systems. It's hard to scale knowledge. It's easy to scale systems and share them with whomever you want.

I learned this lesson the hard way. I knew a lot more than others in my industry and I was still not making the impact or money that I knew I should. Others were giving guys motivational speeches, but not providing anything tangible to get results. I knew I could transform men's lives, but I wasn't reaching the number of men I wanted.

What was holding me back? It was so simple that I overlooked it. I knew my stuff, but the market didn't. If they didn't know about me, how would they be able to access my services and how would I be able to help them?

I had to market myself better but I couldn't market my knowledge. No one cared about how much I knew. What they cared about was how I could help them. So, I turned all my knowledge into systems and that's when my consulting and coaching business started to grow at the rate I wanted.

Bring Uniqueness

Your value comes from doing things that others can't do. What differentiates you from every other guy doing the exact same thing as you? Don't continuously compare yourself to other men because that's a recipe to destroy your self-esteem. I did that for a while and it slowed me down to the point that I almost gave up. But it's a good practice to know the strengths and weaknesses of your competition so that you can navigate your industry effectively.

Find an area of uniqueness that makes you stand out from everyone else. It could be the way you speak, your attire, your expertise, your connections, your personality, or how you lead your teams. Always ask yourself, "Why would anyone else want to do business with me over my competitors?" and, "What makes me stand out from my competitors?"

Combine Skills

Do you know what you're good at? Do you know what you're the best at? By combining two or more skills, you can drive your value as a businessman up even more. The more skills you add, the greater your value.

I'm really good at growing businesses and really good at getting men to perform at their highest potential. I've combined the two to create coaching programs for businessmen. Because I have in-depth expertise in dual areas, businessmen get greater results working with me than with any other coaches.

All good business coaches know business strategies and tactics, but most have limited expertise in personal performance and fulfillment. Good performance coaches know how to get people to perform but they have limited expertise in business strategies and tactics for growth.

Many clients come to me after they've worked with other coaches whose scope is limited. I show men how to be complete and have it all. I've combined the best of both worlds – business and life – and that's what creates unmatched value for the men I work with.

Very few professionals work in the areas that I work on for men such as business or career growth, masculinity, communication, influence, relationships, sex, fatherhood, emotional mastery and fulfillment in life. My favorite is helping men unlock the power of their energy and also the power of their minds. It's taken me decades to get to this point but it was a calculated effort that paid off.

I can count on one hand, the men I'm aware of who are qualified to help family-oriented businessmen at the level I can. I mention this as an example to show you how, by adding more skills to your expertise, you become a more valuable asset. Always think of yourself as an asset that you're constantly improving in value.

Start with an assessment of your skills. Determine what you're good at and what you're really good at. Determine what areas you need to improve. Just because you're not good at something now, doesn't mean you can't be good at it in the future with practice. Skills are like Lego; you can build what you want with them.

Multiply Yourself

There's only one of you and only so much you can do by yourself. Successful businessmen openly share their skills and develop others. A smart businessman multiplies himself by sharing his talent with others. I was afraid to share my expertise with others when I first started my corporate career. I didn't want to lose my competitive advantage. After a few years, I realized that I was holding myself back, so I took the opposite approach. I went from trying to be the best, to helping others become their best. This also forced me to be on top of my own game and not get lazy.

There are two main benefits of multiplying yourself. The most obvious one is that you get more done. The second benefit is even more important. It's the law of reciprocity, or karma in the Indian traditions. The energy you put out eventually comes back to you in some form.

Every week I dedicate a certain number of hours to help men who are facing challenging times. I do it *pro bono*. From time to time, I'll receive a message from some of these men offering to repay me with a new service or product they've developed. Sometimes I really do need what they offer me, so I know that's the universe's way of repaying the energy.

What People Value

Your value comes from what you can do for others. This extends even past the business world. People value different things, but here are the most common that people value and want:

- Save money
- Save time
- Save energy
- Make money
- Achieve more
- Get praise
- Feel secure
- Look good
- Feel special
- Stand out
- Do good work
- Feel a sense of freedom
- Enjoy what they do

- Progress in their roles
- Feel like they belong
- Feel like they make a difference
- Feel appreciated
- Experience a challenge
- Feel fulfilled
- Feel less stress

Moreover, there are two elements that people value beyond all else at this time in history: convenience and hope. The world revolves around convenience and everyone is craving it. The more convenience you provide, the greater your value. Hope is an element that you can never provide enough of. That's why many motivational speakers get paid the big bucks but have no systems to actually help people. People want the hope that their life can get better, and it is going to get better.

Be a Problem Solver

When you're able to solve people's problems, even really big problems, you're at the top of the food chain. Any plumber can install a new toilet in your house. But when your toilet is leaking and flooding your basement, that's when you really value a problem-solving plumber, even when you have to pay him three times as much.

The highest level of being a businessman is teaching others to solve their own problems. When I work with men, I have no desire for them to have to return to me. I don't want to be that chiropractor who tells you to keep coming back to me because you need adjustments. I teach you how to solve your own problems in the future. When the mentee no longer needs the mentor, the mentor has done his job.

Be a Connector

It's always about the "who" more than the "how" or "what." People can help you accelerate your results much faster than any strategy or tactic. Rather than ask yourself "what" you need to do to make it happen, ask yourself "who" can help you make it happen. Because there is someone out there who can help you.

You can also use the concept of "who" to your advantage. You don't need to be an expert yourself in order to be a valuable businessman. I know men who are horrible at business but they have the skill of connecting people. They've built their wealth on who they know.

A connector is almost as valuable as a businessman with skills. If you can't solve someone's problem but you know someone who can, you're an asset. The more people you connect with who have specific skills, the more valuable you become as a businessman. You can become the "go-to" guy just by knowing a bunch of experts.

I'm sure there's that one person you call whenever you need something because they are connected to so many other people. You can be that person in the business world and use your connections to your advantage. My clients always ask me about random stuff that has nothing to do with my expertise because I always find a way to connect them to the right person.

Prioritize

This one is simple. A victorious businessman prioritizes his victories. Take it one step at a time and do it with excellence. Don't confuse excellence with perfection, however. Perfection will hold you back, excellence will move you forward.

Summary Action Items

1. Invest in yourself first.

2. Your profession should provide you income, impact and enjoyment.

3. Be great at marketing yourself.

4. Be the authority and you won't have to worry about money.

5. Be unique and different from your competition.

6. Build on your skills like Lego.

7. Multiply yourself by helping others advance. The universe will pay you back.

8. Provide value to others.

9. Learn to solve problems for others. Teach others how to solve their own problems.

10. Be a connector. The "who" you know is just as important.

11. Prioritize, prioritize, prioritize.

CHAPTER FIFTEEN

Unlocking Genius

"Everybody is a genius. But if you judge a fish by its ability to climb a tree, it will live its whole life believing that it is stupid."
-Albert Einstein (unconfirmed)

In elementary school I had the extreme fortune to have a substitute teacher draw a bunch of circles on the chalkboard and then connect them. He called it a mind map and it was the first time I had heard of the concept. It was also the last time I had a teacher explain the concept to me throughout my entire academic education. My memory is vague but I do remember him talking about the power of the human brain. That moment was the catalyst that really led me to study neuroscience and the power of the human brain.

There was no internet at that time so I had to find whatever books I could on the subject. I did research projects on Leonardo Da Vinci and Einstein and the genius of their insights on the world and the universe. In grade 10, my teacher walked up to my desk and asked why I didn't show up for the awards ceremony the evening before. I explained that I had no reason to. She then let me know that I had won almost every award for my grade; subjects including science, math, English and even in French. She said that I would need a wheelbarrow to take all the awards home.

I didn't understand the importance of that day until later in life.

In high school I walked into my science class as my teacher was marking exams. I had to ask him a question and as I looked down, he came across my exam. He wrote 100% across the top page and moved it to the completed pile. I stopped him and told him that he didn't open the exam to mark it properly. He asked me why he would waste his time going through every question when he knew I got them right.

He said, "Do you want me to go through every question?"

I told him that I did because I wanted to be fair to the other students. So, he went through the questions, then looked up at me and said, "Happy now?"

I became more and more intrigued by the power of the brain. I studied problem solving and creative thinking. I learned how to speed read, memorize, and visualize.

During the rest of high school and the first years of university, I tutored other students. I was the geek, which made me feel special in a way. I could walk into the classroom without studying and score well on the tests. Other skills also improved. Playing basketball on my own in the gym, I could make 30 free throws in a row. I would challenge myself and continuously visualize what I wanted to happen. I thought every kid had that ability, which wasn't really the case.

In my second university year, my study partner and I were quizzing each other for an upcoming final. He asked me question after question and I replied with the exact answer from the textbook. He flipped from one page to the next and said, "You have this whole textbook memorized? It's over 500 pages. You know that's not normal, right?"

That's when it hit me. This wasn't normal.

For the rest of my life, I've outperformed others. I've done this using two principles. One is the principle of work ethic.

Working as hard as I can, but in an intelligent way. The second is the principle of unlocking genius.

Why is Genius Important?

This chapter is particularly important to me and it should be important to you as well. I've experienced the benefits of unlocking genius and they are profound. I attribute most of my success to this principle, and I've seen how it has improved other men's lives as well. It's given them clarity, confidence, and certainty, all which are needed to be a Complete Man and experience complete victory.

The main reason why you aren't getting what you want is because you aren't able to overcome your challenges. If there were no challenges, it would all be smooth sailing. The reason why you can't get over your challenges is because your brain doesn't have convincing solutions. You may actually have solutions but your brain isn't convinced about them. That's why you don't get the results you're looking for.

Unlocking genius gives you solutions to your problems and also creates the sense of certainty that impels you to act and get results. It's a magnetic force that draws you towards it. You can achieve anything you can want in life by harnessing the power of your brain and unlocking this genius energy.

What is Genius?

You and every other person on this planet who has a fully functional brain has the ability to tap into a collective genius. This genius enables you to create your future, solve complex problems, come up with original ideas, and generate endless possibilities. I am not a genius nor do I believe that I am. But at an early age, I was able to tap into strategies for unlocking the power of genius, and I've built on this skill over the years. It's a skill that you can learn. Once you master this skill, you can shape your future rather than just go along with what's handed to you.

You're probably wondering, "What does genius look or feel like?" It's basically a state of coming up with thoughts, ideas, hunches, intuitions or gut feelings that lead you in a direction to overcome challenges and create something new.

Think back to a time where an idea just came to you and it was an instant "ah ha" moment. You had no clue where the thought came from. That's a state of genius. The key is to get control of this state so you can trigger it to happen more often and on command.

You don't have to be super "intelligent" to unlock this genius. Many people have a high IQ but are without creativity or genius. Intelligence may allow you to decode genius a bit easier. Sometimes you can get thoughts, intuitions, or gut feelings and not make any sense of them at first. This is where intelligence can come into play a little.

Genius has stages of evolution and after some practice, you'll remain in the higher stages more often. The stages include the following from lowest to highest:

- **Knowledge** – knowing something conceptually.
- **Expertise** – knowing something to the point that you can play around with it and experiment. You are consciously thinking of new ideas.
- **Intuition** – You can navigate through using hunches and gut feelings. New ideas pop up here and there out of the blue.
- **Zone of genius** – You have ideas and solutions automatically flowing to you. You see things from new and multiple angles. You can see the future clearly, know that it is coming true and it eventually does.

Unlocking Genius

Genius doesn't arise from your conscious mind, primarily because your conscious mind is busy with everyday stimuli: the bills you have to pay, the kids you have to raise, and the daily work that needs to be completed. It's your unconscious mind that is the gateway to genius.

You can't force genius. Trust me, I've tried many times. It's a futile attempt. The more you consciously try, the more you push it away. The key is to allow your brain to fall into a more relaxed state. Stress is the enemy of genius. Optimal stress helps with conscious thinking and problem solving but not with unlocking genius. So, it's vital to remain in a positive, optimistic, and stress-free state. This is non-negotiable for unlocking genius.

When you do unlock genius, there's no mistaking it. It's a feeling of total clarity. Ideas flood your mind. It's as though you can see the future happening right in front of you. Like most creative people, you'll want to keep a notebook handy for writing down all the ideas. I have notebooks in every corner of my house from each washroom to my bedroom. When I'm in the zone, it's like being pregnant, I just want to get the miracle out and into the world.

Meditation

In this section and following section, I'm going to share the methods I use to tap into genius. You can try all of them or a select few. I find that when you combine all of them, you unlock more of the potential of your brain and genius.

The first is meditation. Practice it daily, because it conditions your brain to generate alpha, theta, and even gamma brain waves as you become an experienced meditator. Meditation may take some getting used to at first, but then you'll see that it's unlike anything else you've experienced before.

I use guided meditations, walking meditation, and free flowing mediation. In a guided meditation, music or a voice directs you through a series of meditative levels. Guided meditation is good when you're getting started.

Walking meditation brings on an altered state of consciousness through light, repetitive physical motion. As a child, I practiced walking meditation for a couple of hours each day in my home, walking from the living room through the kitchen to the dining room and back to the kitchen again. I eventually wore a path on the carpet.

Free flowing mediation is my current favorite. You just let your thoughts drift. I find that my mind either goes completely empty or full of ideas. You never know where you'll end up.

Meditation is great but it requires patience. Don't expect to become an instant expert, but over time it can be rewarding and illuminating.

Think and Pause

In this technique, you engage in a total immersion of study and information on a problem or challenge you are trying to overcome. Do this for 30 to 60 minutes maximum. Then go into a dark, quiet room and just relax. Release all tension from your mind and body. As you become fully relaxed, you may find yourself having all sorts of new thoughts and ideas. Just let them flow without judgment. You'll discover at least one or two good ideas for moving forward.

Visualization

Visualization is by far the most powerful tool I've used to create my future. I use this technique with clients not only for unlocking genius, but also to build confidence and emotional strength. Most professional athletes and coaches use visualization. It can help with overcoming any fears or anxieties to build a newer, stronger and better version of yourself.

You can visualize with your eyes open or closed. You can visualize in a highly aroused state of consciousness or in a lower state of arousal. You can visualize in the gym, lifting a weight that's your personal best and feeling all pumped up about it. Or, in a low state of arousal, you visualize lifting the same weight easily and calmly.

Visualization with your eyes closed is easier because many distractions are eliminated. Sight comprises about sixty percent of all your sensory processing. Once you've mastered eyes closed, you can try eyes open visualization. I find it slightly more difficult but the effects are just as good, if not better.

Visualization is a must for unlocking genius. Every day, visualize solutions to specific problems as well as your future in general.

Curiosity & Imagination

Be a boy again. Imagination is the most precious aspect of your consciousness. Yet, it's been torn apart, stomped on, and spat up – and I'm being dramatic for a good reason. I want to call your attention to the fact that conventional educational systems and work environments are designed to create robots of obedience, not genius human beings.

Curiosity is magical. By asking questions, you open your brain to possibility. Statements have simple endings. Questions have endless variations. Instead of thinking that you know something, ask yourself a question instead. Instead of saying "I know what's next," ask yourself, "I wonder what could be next?"

Spend time daydreaming and allow your mind to wander.

During my corporate career, I knew that imagination was a must for my team members. Yet I had to give them permission and train them to use their minds beyond everyday limits.

Please, please, please, if you have young children, encourage their curiosity and imagination. It's one of the most valuable skills they can carry with them through their life.

Meditation, think and pause, visualization, and imagination are ways of making your conscious and unconscious worlds congruent. The following tactics are more practical ways to enhance your creative thinking.

Breaking Patterns

Your brain is built for efficiency, but it gets lazy. It comes to depend on patterns based on information it has received and processed over time. If you stop at a stop sign once or twice, your brain recognizes that the stop sign means stop and you don't even have to think about it next time. Patterns such as this gradually become established at an unconscious level.

You'll always tie your shoes the same way, and you'll most likely tackle problems the same way as well. But as Einstein stated, "We can't solve our problems with the same thinking we used when we created them." Be aware of your thinking patterns. The more conscious you are about how you think, the more you can change how you think. Breaking your patterns will expand your power to come up with solutions.

Speed Reading

The more relevant information you take in, the more information you will have to generate ideas. Geniuses read and they read a lot. But don't be the typical "know it all" who reads hundreds of books and applies nothing. You want to master material, not just skim through it. I read the same book over and over again for one month before I move on. By the time I'm done, I've not only read it, I've absorbed it and fully integrated it.

If you double your reading speed, you double your ability to consume information, so speed reading brings a major return on investment. Many books and software platforms are available to help with this. Speed Reading 7 is one software that I've used.

Memorization

Learn to memorize and avoid allowing technology to make you stupid.

There's a great myth that technology is making us smarter. It's allowing us to gain more information easier and faster but it's not helping us process information any better. It's actually doing the reverse. Remember when you actually knew the phone numbers of all your friends? If you lost your phone now, how many friends would you be able to call?

Your memory allows you to integrate what you've learned into your brain. Otherwise, you'll soon forget it, and what's the point in that? Genius is about proficiency and efficiency, and memorization is a key element for achieving that.

Memorization is not only an essential part of genius but also an essential element to brain health. The older you get, the more you forget. There are people 40 years old who can't remember what they did yesterday. You don't want to be 70 and not be able to remember anything!

Problem Solving

Problem solving is one of the most important skills you can master. The key is to learn how to solve problems in differing ways and using different strategies. A good way to start is to read Ed

De Bono's *Six Thinking Hats*, a great book on facilitation and decision making.

Learn

Be an eternal student and continue to learn new skills throughout your life. Try something new that makes you uncomfortable. If it makes you uncomfortable, it's causing your brain to create new connections. The more connections, the easier it is to come up with new solutions.

Diversify your learning. It's not just reading books. You can learn to play a new instrument, speak a foreign language, or play a new sport. The more diversified your learning, the more diversified your brain becomes and the more diversified you become as a thinking human being.

Sensory Reading and Writing

There is something to be said for reading a physical book and writing on physical paper. Studies show that different neural pathways are activated because you're having a sensory experience that connects different parts of your brain. Reading on a screen and typing on a keyboard don't have the same effects.

From personal experience, my most profound moments of genius come from disconnecting technology and being "old-school" in my approach. That means imagination and a notepad.

Doing the Opposite

Similar to breaking patterns, "doing the opposite" trains you to see things from a new perspective. Instead of brushing your teeth with your right hand, brush with your left. Instead of walking out the front door, walk out the back door. You can even walk about backwards. Making yourself uncomfortable is the whole idea.

Heightening Your Senses

Paradoxically, because we live in a world of sensory overload, our natural senses have become desensitized. You are so bombarded by sights, sounds, and media that your senses are blending everything together. As a result, you overlook images, smells, tastes, sounds and sensations that could help you create better solutions for yourself.

Observation is one of the first steps in creative thinking, yet it is one of the most overlooked. As a teenager, I would dim the lights, watch TV without the sound, and do "silly" things like that to keep my senses from being overstimulated. It actually worked.

Pull back on the stimuli in your environment so that you can truly sense the things around you. The more heightened your senses, the more you can observe and the easier it is to identify things that you've been overlooking. Plus, life becomes a lot more pleasurable from a sensory experience perspective.

Creativity Time

Setting aside time for creativity on a daily basis creates a habit of creative thinking. Although genius doesn't always come based on your schedule, you can train yourself to tap into it more frequently. Plan a period in your day when you are in a good mood and full of energy. Schedule no more than 60 mins. This should be a time of free flowing, unforced ideas.

Sleep

For several important reasons, sleep is critical for your brain performance. Sleep allows what you've learned during the day to be consolidated in your brain. It transitions short-term memory into long-term memory. Most importantly, the moments before you fall asleep and right after you wake up are the perfect states of minds for your genius to unlock. I try to nap once a day, not because I'm tired but to capture this opportunity for unlocking genius.

Summary Action Items

1. Your unconscious mind is the gateway to genius.

2. Allow genius to flow through you.

3. Meditate.

4. Visualize solutions to your problems as well as your future.

5. Be curious and use your imagination.

6. Break your existing thinking patterns.

7. Learn to speed read.

8. Learn to memorize.

9. Get good at problem solving.

10. Keep learning new things.

11. Read, read, read. Try reading physical books and writing on paper when possible.

12. Do the opposite of what you're used to.

13. Tone down the stimuli around you to heighten your senses.

14. Schedule daily creativity time.

15. Sleep well as it's important for brain function.

CHAPTER SIXTEEN

Sacrifice & Suffering

"Accept your situation, not the outcome."

-Unknown

Growing up on an orchard was fun but it came with challenges. I had severe allergies to grass, dust, and pollen. When the month of May came, I could barely breathe. I would be out in the orchard for ten or more hours in the sun, with a constant flow of fluids running down my nose and face. I don't know how many tissues I went through in a day. I would be constantly sneezing and trying to catch my breath. It felt like getting punched in the face and being sat on by a bear at the same time. The minute I would sit in the vehicle on the drive home, I would pass out from the exhaustion.

Even my parents, who always expected 110% from me, would even tell me to take a break. But I wouldn't allow an "allergy" to get the best of me. It wasn't even a thing; it was just a term given to how I reacted to tiny spores and dust particles. It seemed silly to allow that to control my outcomes.

I reached a point where I could block out the allergy if I concentrated enough. It wasn't a permanent solution but it got me through. Eventually, I decided to get allergy shots as I didn't want to be sitting in university classes sneezing my head off.

Because excavators were expensive to rent or hire, we dug

irrigation ditches with shovels. It was the worst work ever. I would look down the field to see how much further we would have to dig and it seemed endless. There were boulders that took hours to remove. We used long crowbars and sledge-hammers to remove and break them.

My uncle was the lead and he was determined to do the job well. Others would say to go around the rocks but he said dig them up to keep the lines straight. He was no stranger to hard work. He spent his early days as a man in India cutting grains for the cows with machinery that was hand-powered. His hands were so strong that he could crush an apple in his hand like it was nothing.

I was the youngest in the crew but I wasn't going to let him down. I kept pushing and pushing myself. Sometimes I asked the older men to take a break so I could continue. I was only a teen but my uncle would tell me that I worked like a man. For him to say that meant the world to me. I worked so hard those summers that my fingernails fell off from bashing the shovel against the rocks day after day.

I was surrounded by strong men that wouldn't accept defeat and neither would I. It was almost an addiction to see how far I could push myself. I realized that if I could push myself further and further, nothing in my external world would be able to hold me down. I purposefully put rocks in my shoes and walked around with the pain all day. I would use a hand saw rather than a chainsaw to cut large branches so I could tell myself I did it. I would carry fertilizer bags as far as I could to exhaust myself and build up my stamina, and my character too.

The Illusion

Is suffering a natural part of life, or is it not natural to suffer? Chances are that you've felt major heartache or pain in your life already. It could be from an injury you've faced, a loved one who's died, or having the woman of your dreams leave you for someone else. Some event in your life has caused you to experience severe suffering.

The truth is, thoughts and emotions that you connect to an experience are what create the suffering. In some cultures, death is a celebration. In others it's a complete tragedy. The same event with totally different reactions.

How you react has a great deal to do with how you were conditioned to react. In the Indian culture, if a husband dies, it's almost expected that the widow will react in a hysteric fit of screaming and shouting while she pounds on his chest. If she keeps her poise, she's seen as uncaring.

The difference between pain and suffering is the length of time. If your buddy just found out that his wife was cheating on him, you'll see him as a guy who is going through significant pain and anguish. When you see him months later at a party and he's still acting the same way, you tell yourself that he's suffering from a broken heart. His pain is transitioned into suffering. Buddhists view resistance to pain as the cause of suffering: suffering = pain + resistance. When you acknowledge the pain, accept it and move forward, you can free yourself of the suffering.

Much suffering comes from thinking of the future or the past; the moments that you'll no longer have or the moments that you will never have. If a loved one passes away, you think of the moments you had or wanted to have, and that you'll never have again.

I know this feeling. When my father passed, I felt it deeply. I wanted him to see my children grow and I wanted my children to experience having their grandfather around. My dad adored his grandkids and I wish they would've experienced that love for many years to come. But that's not going to happen and I've come to terms with it. The event of my dad passing was just a moment in time. Everything else is being created in my mind.

Pain is finite in the location or the situation or time period. A pain in your lower back has a specific location. But you may associate that pain with other aspects of your life, like not being able to sit for long periods or travel long distances. The pain is broadened by your mind and emotions. If not contained, the pain eventually becomes suffering.

Pain is a sensation and the meaning that you assign to the sensation is what matters. If your pain is there to help you learn and grow, that's an empowering meaning. If your pain is there to punish you or make you feel unworthy, it's a disempowering meaning. Pain is energy and energy is a form of communication. What is this energy telling you? What can you learn from this energy? By taking the approach of curiosity rather than anguish, you'll notice that the pain isn't as bad you think.

The Norm

Some men just wallow in suffering and I feel sorry for them. It's a way for them to connect with themselves. Because they don't feel joy in their life, feeling something is better than nothing.

Is it easier to feel suffering than to feel joyful? If we see a man who looks too happy, we think there's something wrong with him. Turn on the news and you'll see suffering everywhere. Suffering shouldn't not be the norm, but it is for many men.

Suffering is a choice and you have full control over this choice. I acknowledge that you may be feeling pain, but do not allow the pain to become your suffering. Choose to see beyond the pain, and you'll see that the pain is only a small fraction of your overall life.

When you can't see beyond the pain, you allow suffering to win. I know that's not something you want. Tell yourself now that you are the victor, that you will not bow down to your pain.

Suffering can be a rite of passage for men. It can mean enduring a strenuous situation or event that causes you to push yourself beyond your current limits as a man. Suffering can turn you into a man you never knew you could become. However, there is a limit and prolonged suffering is never the answer.

I see this quite often and I even experienced it myself. Do you tell yourself that you are suffering for the betterment of someone else? Perhaps you're staying in a miserable marriage to keep your family together. You're sacrificing your own happiness for the happiness of your children. How long will that last? What will your children think of this? Well, they may think that suffering is the way life has to be. But it doesn't.

Suffering, whether just or unjust is not meant to be permanent. A victor sees suffering as a challenge that he will get past and conquer. A victim sees suffering as a part of him and bathes in it. Suffering is the norm for an inComplete Man.

Dealing with Pain

Whether your pain is mental, physical or emotional, the methods to deal with them are relatively similar. First, always seek help from a professional. They are trained and are considered experts for a reason. They have knowledge that the average person doesn't.

Over the years I've learned techniques from my grandfather, spiritual practices as well as ancient teachings on how to overcome pain. Below is how I personally deal with pain:

- **Accept it** – When you first feel the pain, acknowledge it and accept that you're feeling it.
- **Pinpoint it** – Outline where the pain is located and its finite aspects. Is it based in a specific location, time period

or event? The more precise you can be, the less it will spread.

- **Separate yourself** – Understand that you are not your pain. Pain is only a sensation that is fixed to an event, situation or body part. It's not you.
- **Remove resentment** – Remove the resentment for the cause of the pain. The less resentment, the faster you heal.
- **Learn** – Pain is a teacher. What is the meaning for this pain? What are you meant to learn from it? How can you grow from this pain? What advantage does this pain give you? The more you learn, the stronger you become.
- **Face it** – Don't shy away from the pain and face it head on. The more you avoid it, the stronger it becomes and the weaker you become.
- **Wisdom council** – Ask the wisest people on your Wisdom Council what they would do. I explain what this council is in a later chapter.
- **Envision your future** – See yourself beyond the pain and imagine what your life will be like once you've overcome it.
- **Give and receive love** – Love is the ultimate healer. It's also the easiest way to overshadow pain.
- **Laugh** – The simplest yet most effective way to stop pain is to laugh. Find reasons to laugh and laugh daily.
- **Get help** – If you want to overcome the pain faster or it becomes greater or you're not able to manage it or it's turning into suffering, always seek help.

It's a Choice

Suffering is a choice and you are in control of your choices. The only time you don't is if you're locked in a prison and confined to your cell. Even then, you have a choice just as Nelson Mandela demonstrated after spending 27 years in prison. He spent his time in prison learning and growing, which allowed him to become President of South Africa after he was released. The majority of men would have crumbled, but he chose not to.

Options create choices and choices create control of your pain and suffering. If you want to remove suffering from your life, create more options. You are never locked down to a single path although it may seem like it at times.

There were times in my life that I felt like I had no options. When my marriage was failing, I felt trapped. Even though I taught the practice of creating options, I temporarily overlooked my own. One of my colleagues reminded me of my options, and a light went on in my mind. After, my marriage changed almost immediately.

When you're faced with adversity, pain, or suffering, write down three to five options. Two options aren't ideal because it leads to a black-or white, this-or-that, all-or-nothing perspective. Anything over five and it becomes overwhelming for your brain to effectively decide. Too many options aren't necessarily better.

Sacrificing for Success

Men are taught that we must sacrifice for the greater good. We're also taught that the greater the sacrifice, the greater the reward. If you want to be super successful, you must endure sacrificing your personal happiness. But those principles are not universally valid, they are situationally valid.

According to Aristotle, the Greek philosopher who mentored Alexander the Great, happiness is one of the main purposes of life. Therefore, why suspend your happiness for the sake of happiness? Logically, that doesn't make sense.

There are some benefits to short-term sacrifice. If you sacrifice your happiness now at some level, it can allow you to have greater happiness in the future. For example, removing donuts from your life now will allow you to slim down and wear your clothes more comfortably. If being able to wear the clothes you want will make you happier than eating donuts right now, then it's an empowering sacrifice.

If you have been sacrificing for a long period of time or to a great degree and not seeing the results you want, it's time to reevaluate. What are you sacrificing for? Will it bring you happiness in the future? Are you setting a good example for others? Remember that extended sacrifice is suffering.

It's easy to self-justify your sacrifice. Your mind rationalizes what it believes to be true. It's also easy for you to be influenced. You may hear stories of other men who sacrificed and as a result, they attained success. The problem with this thinking is that you are not those men and you are not living their life. Although your situations may look similar, they are not exactly the same.

It's also important to ask yourself who else your sacrifice impacts? Is it fair for others around you to be impacted by your sacrifice? How is this impacting your wife and kids? If you're a man who spends evenings and weekends working, you may have to ask yourself some tough questions. Are you really doing it for them or are you doing it for yourself? Are you justifying it by saying that you're doing it for others?

Do you really need to sacrifice in order to achieve success? Well, it depends on what you consider to be sacrifice. For one man, restraining from eating donuts may be torture. For another, it may be nothing at all. Your sacrifice is yours alone. It shouldn't be compared to someone else's.

Attaining a goal for the sake of attaining the goal is short-lived. But the character you build along the way lasts your entire lifetime. What character are you building?

Discipline vs Suffering

Based on the Bhagavad Gita, an ancient Hindu scripture, discipline is the ultimate path to joy. Discipline should not be seen as suffering, as suffering leads to pain. Discipline leads to growth and progress. The Gita refers to the term "yoga" as an expression of discipline. The term yoga stems from the Sanskrit term "yuj" which means "to unite." By practicing discipline, you become one with discipline.

Discipline can also create freedom, because you are using your own free will and internal spirit to practice it. You are not enslaved by external desires. You choose your actions and your path whereas many men are forced to have their actions chosen for them. Freedom is the gateway to joy. Without freedom, there is no joy. Discipline leads to freedom, which leads to joy.

My grandfather taught me these principles as a young man. He was the most disciplined man I knew. He woke up every morning at the exact same time to do his prayers. He followed his daily disciplines without fault. The only thing that eventually held him back was his health conditions. Even then, he continued as much as his body would allow. From his strength, I learned to attain mine.

But my grandfather was also very clear that unnecessary suffering was absurd. He said, "There is no pride in suffering." For my grandfather to say that was a big deal for me. He was a very proud man. Men have egos and the ego can push a man to suffer rather than practice discipline. There is a fine line between discipline and suffering that you must be aware of.

Summary Action Items

1. Accept your situation but not your outcome.

2. Accept the pain, don't resist it and then allow it to pass. Resistance creates suffering.

3. Follow the principles in this chapter for overcoming pain.

4. Create three to five options when faced with adversity. Options create choice and choice gives you control over pain and suffering.

5. Ask yourself if your suffering is really worth it? How is it impacting others?

6. Short-term sacrifice may be needed. Long-term sacrifice must be questioned.

7. Discipline creates freedom and joy. Discipline is not sacrifice.

CHAPTER SEVENTEEN

Addictions

"Recovery is hard, regrets are harder."
-Brittany Burgunder

My dad was addicted to alcohol from the age of 15. Since my grandfather was in the military and only home two months out of the year, he left my dad in the care of his younger brother. My dad's uncle suffered from alcoholism himself and passed his addiction to my dad.

My grandfather and his brother were complete opposites. Being the sons of a spiritual and religious teacher, you would think that they would've turned out with similar beliefs, but they didn't. Both of them were military men. My grandfather was very disciplined, moral, and rational. His brother was not. My grandfather rarely drank, his brother drank every day.

My dad enlisted in the Indian police force at age 17 and was a police officer for seven years. The discipline of the police kept him from indulging in too much alcohol during that period. When he immigrated to Canada, he had free rein. I saw the man I called "dad" transform into a man I couldn't bear to be around. He became a completely different person when he drank. He transitioned from his masculine identity into a state of desperation. My grandfather would tell me how an addiction could turn a strong man into a weak man in minutes. I could see the pain my grandfather felt when he saw my dad drink.

For my entire life, I watched my dad try to quit drinking but then get sucked back in. At times he would drink for five days straight. He would have bottles hidden everywhere. My mom would find them and hide them but my dad would go out and buy more. He liked the hard stuff too. Beer was too weak for him, a "lady's drink."

My dad would have remorse on his face when he woke up the next morning not knowing what happened the night before. I was angry at him but the more I learned about how the brain operates, I realized that addictions are a disease. Aside from drinking, my dad was an awesome guy. All my friends loved him. He would just say things openly, which is fairly rare in the Indian culture. He was traditional, yet liberal. He knew what his sons were up to but also told us to keep a good head on our shoulders.

Outside of drinking, my dad lived a fairly healthy life. He was very physically active, and most of his food was from his home garden. However, his alcohol escalated his diabetes, which can kill the nerves in your feet. My dad was close to the point of not being able to walk. A doctor said the nerve damage was irreversible but somehow after he stopped drinking for several months, he was back to normal.

He also had a minor heart attack. A stent was put in, which forced him to stay sedentary for a few months. He stopped drinking, and again he recovered. My dad's nickname was Lucky and it made sense. He survived a lot of things throughout his life. Maybe he thought he was invincible. If nerve damage, diabetes, and a heart attack couldn't kill him, what could?

He was a good man, but good men can still have addictions.

What is an Addiction?

In simplest terms, an addiction can be defined as something that you cannot control or have trouble controlling. It can be a behavior, or even a thought.

I'm not a professional therapist, so please consult a professional if you are dealing with an addiction. I think of addiction from a softer and wider perspective than others might. Addictions don't have to be dangerous, like drugs or alcohol. They can be as simple as biting your nails or staying in a certain emotional pattern. Some men are addicted to feeling bad about themselves. Others are addicted to being arrogant.

You may not even know that you're addicted, and feel it's a normal part of life. For example, there are a lot of coffee addicts out there. Many addictions are unconscious as almost half of your life is based on habits. Are you aware of your addictions?

The Science of Addiction

Addiction resides in both your body and your brain. You feel it in your body but it's being programmed in your mind. Each time you perform a behavior, you hardwire neurons together. It's like carving a path through a forest. The first pass through, you may cut down a tree here or there. The second time, you cut a few more and each time after that until the path is completely clear. You've created a clear pathway for that behavior so it's easier to do the next time.

Dopamine is a neurotransmitter in your brain that plays a significant role in motivation, learning, and your brain's reward system. Dopamine is released each time you perform a pleasurable act. It's a powerful chemical that motivates you to do, learn, and repeat behavior.

An addiction alters the dopamine uptake and absorption in your brain. You then need more of the same addictive trigger to get the same degree of pleasure. Eventually, you crave the addictive trigger more than the feeling of pleasure itself. Soon, you do things that are otherwise completely out of your character.

An addiction is a disease of the brain. It's not the person's "fault" although they do have a choice regarding how to deal with it. Some men just don't know how. I don't blame my dad for his addiction because he just didn't know how to overcome it.

Emotional Reasons for Addictions

There are many reasons why men have addictions. It would be unjust to judge a man based primarily on his addiction. It's important to look behind the addiction to see what his character truly is.

Based on my personal experience in dealing with men who have addictions, I have found that there's a range of reasons for their behavior:

- **Feeling incomplete** – The substance or act helps you fill a void.
- **Freedom** – The substance or act allows you to be more like yourself. This is common with drugs and alcohol.
- **Stress release** – The substance or act relieves your stress temporarily.
- **Escape from reality** – You're tired of your life and you want to escape.
- **Boredom** – The substance or act allows you to feel more excitement or have variety in your life.
- **Need excitement** – You need excitement so you need to be stimulated all the time.
- **Something new** – You want to try something new and you get hooked.
- **Feel like a badass** – The act makes you feel like you're doing something you shouldn't which creates excitement or attention for you.
- **It feels good** – The substance or act makes you feel good.

- **Piss others off** – You do it to spite others.
- **Get attention** – You do something you know you shouldn't be doing to get attention from others.
- **Numb pain** – You're feeling mental, emotional, physical or even spiritual pain and you want to numb it.
- **Feel in control** – You're addicted to something that makes you feel in control.

Regardless of the reasons, most men are embarrassed by their addictions. They don't openly go around telling people that they are addicts unless they are addicted to getting attention or they're crying out for help. Some will go to great lengths to hide their addiction. Many will even deny it. Denying is another way of hiding it.

Technology

Bear with me on my technology rant. Technology has helped move the world further in so many ways. Less fortunate people around the globe are in a better place because of technology. However, I personally think that certain technology is ruining the lives of many people in many ways.

Much of today's technology is created as a distraction from reality. Technology ought to enhance your productivity and enjoyment of life. But I see men having less time and diminished enjoyment of their lives.

Many more people are addicted to their smartphones than alcohol and drugs. Walk down the street and you'll see what I'm talking about. I was downtown Toronto one day and I counted how many people were on their phones even while they were engaging with their friends or colleagues. Eight out of ten people I observed were on their phones, and not just for a quick second. They were immersed in their smartphones.

I observed a group of ten friends sitting in a circle and all of them were on their phones. I'd like to say that this is not the norm but I'm afraid it is. You can go into any restaurant and see a couple texting others while ignoring each other. Or you can see parents giving their kids iPads or iPhones just to keep them busy. Disney even conducted a study that showed the number one factor impacting the children's experience in the theme parks was their parents being on smartphones.

It seems like people are so bored with reality that they are addictively seeking an easy escape. This is the opposite of how a mindful alpha lives. You can of course use a smartphone but don't allow it to use you.

I was once on a video conference call with a prominent high tech, international entrepreneur. Speaking of a new app he was designing, he said, "I want people to get addicted to this." I don't think he even knew that he said that. He was so deeply into technology that he was blind to its impact. From then on, I stopped associating with him and removed all his products and services from my business.

I support technology but I do not support technology for personal gain at the expense of people or society. I know entrepreneurs who sell services online but won't allow their own children to use those services because they know it can mess them up. Technology companies are profiting in the billions while individuals, couples and children are negatively impacted. Because technology has advanced so rapidly in the last two decades, we don't have conclusive evidence on long-term impact on people's physical and mental health.

Social media isn't making us more social. It's making us less social. It's easy to get addicted. I had to ban myself from Instagram after I watched a clip of a lion hunting a boar. My feed was instantly flooded with animals slaughtering each other. Social media companies spend billions on developing algorithms first to get you hooked, and then to profit from you. If you think they're doing it for any other purpose, think again.

Good Addictions

Are all addictions equal? I don't believe they are. I think some are good for you if they empower you to be a better man, achieve your goals, and do good for others. I'm addicted to working out, reading, learning, and sometimes sex. They are just part of who I am.

Unless I'm physically hurt, I don't allow anything from stopping me from working out. I have books and notepads all over my house. My wife tells me I should chill more but that is my way of chilling. I love it because it helps me help others. I've also got a great wife who indulges my pleasures in the bedroom. She doesn't mind because I'm having sex with her and not with other women.

Moderation and Flexibility

It's okay to live in extremes as long as you know how to moderate and be flexible. If you continuously live in extremes and it's not benefiting you or anyone else, why are you doing it? Even the best athletes eventually retire. They live in extremes while they are pros but they know that there's a time to move on. They pursue business ventures, spend time with family, or just enjoy life. You can't go 100 miles per hour forever. You're bound to crash.

The Roman stoics believed that we are creatures of desire but we have rational minds for a reason. It's human nature to satisfy a desire, but the secret is to live in moderation. Don't allow the extremes to control you. That's addiction.

Rigidity creates cracks. Flexibility enables growth. Being

strong and rigid are not the same thing. The strongest towers in New York are those that can withstand the winds. They are able to shift with the wind so that they don't crack and fall over. They stay strong by being flexible. The same applies to you in your habits and addictions. Change isn't always easy but when you see it as flexibility, it's a little easier to handle.

Overcoming an Addiction

Can you get over an addiction? Yes, but you may need a helping hand. That's why I recommend reaching out to a professional.

Addictions can be overridden but not removed from your brain. Once that path has been carved through the forest, it will always be there. That's why it's easy for men to relapse into the same addiction. The secret is to create new paths that are less destructive and have a better reward at the end. Rather than eating junk food, get addicted to working out. Rather than jerking off to porn all the time, have lots of sex with your wife. Trade your disempowering addictions for empowering ones.

Summary Action Items

1. Have empathy for yourself and others who may have an addiction. It's not them, it's their brain.

2. Help others who have an addiction. They need it.

3. Avoid getting addicted to technology. Others are getting richer while your life is getting poorer.

4. Get addicted to "stuff" that empowers you.

5. Learn the art of moderation and flexibility.

6. To overcome an addiction, create a more empowering addiction that's good for you.

7. Always seek professional help if you have an addiction that you can't get over.

PART THREE

The Fulfillment Framework

The Fulfillment Framework is a system for experiencing life to the fullest, with peace, joy, and love. If you feel like any of these qualities are lacking in your life – if you're just not as happy as you want to be – the Fulfillment Framework will enable you to quickly change that.

The Fulfillment Framework = Thoughts + Feelings + Energy

CHAPTER EIGHTEEN

Your Thoughts

"Change your thoughts and you change your world."
-Norman Vincent Peale

In my third year of university, I transferred from my hometown university to a larger one about 240 miles away, in Vancouver. I made the move in order to be closer to my girlfriend at that time. It was a big transition. I went from a campus with 2,000 students that was a seven-minute drive from home to one with 40,000 students which I reached by an hour's ride on public transportation.

The first semester was the toughest for me. I had virtually no friends on campus and had courses scheduled from 9:00 am to sometimes 10:00 pm, Monday to Friday. Plus, it would rain for weeks in Vancouver and sometimes I didn't see the sun for days. I'm a sun person and I need it to function properly.

I also went from living in a nice home to renting a dreary and tiny basement suite with very few windows and light. All of these changes were getting to me fast.

A few weeks into my first semester, I started to sleep in on the weekends. That wasn't like me at all. I would often eat two McChicken sandwiches and two super-sized fries at McDonalds after getting off by a bus at 11:00 pm. In four months I gained close to 40 pounds. I fell into the habit of sleeping through entire weekends, getting up only to shower and eat.

I nitpicked everything that wasn't going right. I told myself the campus was too large because I had to run from one class to the next. I disliked sitting in an auditorium with 500 other students instead of 50. I hated taking public transport because it took three times as long to get to campus. But I didn't want to drive my car and pay for parking and still have to walk for 20 minutes to reach the campus. My girlfriend lived 45 minutes away and I didn't have time to see her during the week. Yet, I would sleep through the weekends.

One negative thought led to the next. It became a vicious cycle leading to a state of depression. In four months, I changed from a guy who loved life, who was outgoing and active, to someone who was overweight, inactive, and sleeping his life away.

When I realized that I was technically suffering from depression, I made the commitment to overcome it. I researched everything I could find about depression and came to one conclusion. I had to change my thoughts. My thoughts caused me to be miserable, not my situation. To get back to normal and overcome this, I would have to change my thoughts.

I had found the first element of The Fulfillment Framework. Within three months, I lost all the weight, was even in better shape than before, got back to being me and started loving life again.

Your Life Starts with Your Thoughts

Philosophers like Buddha (Buddhist philosopher) and Marcus Aurelius (the Roman emperor and Stoic philosopher) spoke about the power of thoughts and the mind thousands of years ago. They shared the principle that the origin of your world is your thoughts. Everything you have or don't have is based on how you think and what you think. Having consistent negative thoughts creates frustration and anger. On the flip side, positive and optimistic thoughts lead to better outcomes, true fulfillment, and completeness.

I'm a firm believer that our thoughts are the basis of our reality. Two people, for example, can be in identical situations but they will experience those situations differently based on their thoughts. The difference may be slight, or it may be drastic. The experiences of both people are real, because how you think about your reality, literally is your reality; how they perceive their reality is their reality.

Hundreds of placebo studies show that if patients think they are getting a treatment that will heal them, they are just as likely to be healed as if they had gotten the actual treatment. They heal themselves by thinking they are getting healed.

The easiest way to not get what you want is to not think about it. If you don't want a better career, don't think about having a better career. If you don't want more free time, don't think about having more free time. If you don't want a passionate relationship, don't think about having a passionate relationship. Very rarely will you get something you want without having a thought about it first. Everything you have starts with a thought, even if it's an unconscious thought.

Your True Alpha

Your thoughts are your true alpha, the origin and creation of your life. Everything you want in your life starts with a thought first. Your first thought is a spark that lights other sparks, and eventually those sparks create a fire. The more you fuel this fire, the more you generate creative and persistent ways to overcome your challenges.

The initial thought alone doesn't lead to creation. You need to be consistent with your thoughts. Obstacles will get in your way, and it's your consistent thoughts that allow you to break through them.

Studies have shown that a person's thoughts impact emotions and then thoughts combined with their emotions impact their behavior. A person's behavior then impacts their environment and their environment responds accordingly.

Imagine your employee telling you that they messed up an important deal with a client and your company is going to lose $1 million as a result. How will you react to the situation?

Will you fire your employee and beg your client for forgiveness? Will you coach your employee how to recover from the mistake and show them how to rebuild the relationship with your client? Will you forget about it all together and move on to find another client?

All these scenarios could lead to different outcomes based on how your client reacts to you and how you react to your client's next moves. All of these events come to fruition from your thoughts.

The Less Fortunate

I hate watching people suffer who don't deserve it, whether it's the homeless in my local area or starving children around the world. Are their thoughts creating their reality? Are they creating their own suffering? I cannot answer this with confidence. Every time I think about it, I get so emotional that I don't want to think about it any further. By no means do I imagine that people purposely ask to suffer to such a high degree.

A successful entrepreneur once told me his story. He was homeless as a young adult and he said that the worst thing about being homeless wasn't the fact that he didn't have access to food or shelter. Countless people walked by and pretended like he was invisible. He felt like he didn't exist. I'm sharing this story with you because it touched me so deeply. Instead of giving the home-less money, which I had done in the past, I give them money and acknowledgement that they do exist to me.

I cannot say that every person who is suffering from star-vation, disease or misfortune has brought it upon themselves as an individual. However, I do believe that as a collective group of human beings, our thoughts have created these realities. If we haven't created them directly, we definitely haven't helped solve them. There is much work to be done with people and their suffering.

Some people constantly play the victim, blame others, and always look at the downside of everything. As a result, they have poor relationships, are financially unstable and it seems like nothing goes their way. I'm sure you know these people. They are the ones who get nowhere because they do very little going any-where else. There is no doubt in my mind that these individuals do create their unfortunate circumstances.

The Science Behind Thoughts

As much as scientists know about thoughts, there's a lot more that they don't know. Thought is produced by a neuron (or number of neurons) in your brain reaching an action potential (electrical threshold) that causes a signal to pass through it and trigger other neurons. These neurons produce a thought. But they still don't know how a thought is created.

You probably know the story of Aladdin and his magic lamp. Rub the lamp, and a genie appears. But why and how does that genie appear? What is the genie made of and where does that magic come from? The same questions apply to our thoughts. We know that neurons firing create a thought, but not why that thought appears. It's beyond magic, and even science can't ex-plain it.

Your imagination can create similar "magic" reactions in your brain. Your brain cannot tell the difference between what you are imagining and what's actually happening. Have you experienced a dream that seemed so real that you swore it happened for real? That's what I'm talking about. Your brain is an amazing organ and the more scientists learn about it, the more mysterious it seems.

The Brain, Mind and Thoughts

I refer to the brain, the mind, and thoughts as three distinct entities, because there are basic differences.

The brain is just like any other organ. It's made of cells and has a function that's evolved over millions of years. If you think of your brain as hardware in a computer, it's interesting that your brain hasn't been updated for close to 200,000 years. Your brain has a very similar structure and hardwiring to a human living 200,000 years ago.

Your mind is the combination of your brain and the pre-programmed software that comes along with it. Think of your mind as your computer, including both hardware and software. Your software also hasn't been updated much over the past 200,000 years. Yet the way humans live has dramatically changed since then. You're living in modern times with ancient software.

Your thoughts, both conscious and unconscious, are what your mind produces, like a word document or a pdf produced by your computer. But it's important to understand that, while your thoughts are a product of your mind, you are more than your thoughts. You are a conscious being and a source of energy. Having great thoughts, doesn't make you a great person. Having bad thoughts doesn't make you a bad person. You are deeper than your thoughts.

Men have asked me if they are crazy because they've had the

thought of doing something they wouldn't normally do. Maybe you want to play a nasty prank on your neighbor. Or maybe there is a brief moment that you wish you didn't have kids. That doesn't make you a bad neighbor or father. It just means that your mind is producing wild thoughts. It's your actions that really count. My rule of thumb is: as long as it doesn't hurt you, others, living creatures and the planet, go for it.

Unconscious vs Conscious Thoughts

Thoughts are powerful but they are also elusive. Neuroscientists have not determined the exact number of thoughts a person produces but estimates are from 10,000 to 80,000 thoughts per day. Some neuroscientists believe that over 90% of your thoughts are unconscious. If so, your unconscious brain has more influence over you than you think.

The brain has been designed to optimize energy usage. If your brain were to process every single thought with your full conscious awareness, that would require amazing mental energy. Imagine having to think about every step you take or movement you make. You wouldn't have thinking capacity left to do anything that required real thought.

Instead, your brain creates patterns based on your previous experiences. Thoughts that are not important enough to be conscious are kept at an unconscious level. John Bargh, a social psychologist at Yale University, calls this process automaticity, which has four characteristics:

- You might not be aware of the mental process that is happening.
- You might not be involved in the initiation of the mental process.
- The process involves low level tasks requiring low mental resources.

- You may not have the ability to alter or stop the process once it's started.

Automaticity can be extremely useful. But what if your kids walk up to you when you're working and ask you to play and your automatic response is, "Not now, I'm busy." That's not what they want or deserve to hear. Where in your life do you need to be more intentional?

Don't underestimate your unconscious thoughts. Think of them as the backstage crew in the Cirque Du Soleil performance. They are the guys and gals who make the props, set up the stages and train the performers. They are the magic behind the curtains.

I would argue that the backstagers have an even bigger role than the performers themselves. Your conscious thoughts are a product of your unconscious thoughts. Hunches, intuitions, and those moments where you have a flash of brilliance are made possible by your unconscious.

The challenges that are consciously evident are the easy ones to deal with. It's the invisible challenges, the ones in your unconscious, that are really holding you back. You may be able to uncover these yourself, or you may need assistance from a professional coach to help bring them to light.

Taking Control of Your Mind

Your consistent thoughts lead to actions. If your life expressed all your thoughts, you'd be living in ten different cities, with 14 wives, 49 mistresses, and five different careers. Your consistent thoughts lead to your actions, whether they are empowering or disempowering.

Your task is to take control of your conscious thoughts in order to build habits (automaticity) that enable your unconscious mind to work in your favor.

Restructuring your brain and its neural connections requires you to use your conscious thoughts with intention. You really can create new brain neurons, which is called neurogenesis, and you can also create new connections within your brain. Scientists previously believed that the brain couldn't change very much. But studies now show that you can modify your brain to a certain degree to better suit your life. For example, a prominent study of taxi drivers showed that the part of their brain responsible for learning and memory (hippocampus) was larger than the average person's. There is some debate whether these people were taxi drivers because they had better memory skills to start with, but that's not as likely.

Here are a few ways to take control of your mind. The first is to keep learning. The more you learn, the more neural connections you create. Second is meditating. Studies show that meditating 12 minutes a day can help you sleep better, have greater focus, calm your anxiety, perform better and improve your memory. The third is to protect your unconscious brain. Use your conscious thoughts and actions as a filter. Stay away from the negative garbage you're exposed to throughout the day.

Thoughts, even unconscious thoughts, can become habits. What habits do you need to modify and what habits you need to get rid of completely? You want to ensure that your new habits stick and that requires strong neural connections. Neuroscientists have identified six factors for creating stronger neural connections: increasing frequency through greater repetition; amplifying the habit with more intensity; integrating all five of your senses into the habit; creating novelty with your habits so your brain remains curious; making it personal to you; focusing on the reward.

Thoughts and Emotions

Thoughts (both conscious and unconscious) and emotions are highly intertwined. It's almost impossible for you to feel great and have negative thoughts at the exact same time. When you feel like your life is great, your thoughts are aligned with that feeling. When you feel like your life has hit rock bottom, your thoughts are aligned with that as well. Your thoughts are a catalyst for your feelings and are aligned with your feelings most of the time.

There is one exception to this rule. You can train your brain to a point that even if you're feeling low, you can still have positive and empowering thoughts without faking it. It's like a muscle. The more you train it, the stronger it becomes. An important first step towards fulfillment and completeness is realizing that you have full control over your mind and thoughts.

Summary Action Items

1. Take control of your thoughts instead of your brain taking control.

2. Use your thoughts to create the life you want.

3. Don't feel guilty for having crazy thoughts. It's your actions that count.

4. Use your conscious thoughts to build better unconscious habits.

5. Use your conscious thoughts to protect your unconscious mind.

6. Learn continuously, to upgrade your mind and your brain.

CHAPTER NINETEEN

Mastering Your Feelings

"Your feelings, not your logic, lead you to a more complete life."

-Purdeep Sangha

As a child, I spent a lot more time with the women in my family than the men. I was sensitive and would always worry about others. I also had an affinity towards animals, especially the strays or injured animals in our neighborhood. My parents knew that if there was an injured animal around, I'd be bringing it home. If there was a stray, I'd be knocking on everyone's doors trying to find it a home.

As I got older, I noticed that I became more and more emotional. I was a typical teenager who did typical things for the most part. But I always had this deep-rooted compassion for people and animals. If my parents asked me to put rat poison out in the orchard, I couldn't do it. They would be upset with me because the gophers would chew up the roots of the cherry and apple trees. I tried my best not to hurt others whether that was a person or any other living being.

I got into a fight with a kid in high school because he kept calling me "Paki" and I finally told him to piss off. I gave him a black eye but I felt horrible for months. My mom still reminds me of how remorseful I was.

In my twenties, things changed. I was fully into academics and then into the corporate world. I went from operating from my emotions to operating more from logic. It didn't help that all my colleagues called me the "smart guy." I started to believe that being smart and logical was the best way to operate successfully.

At the same time, I was going through challenges in my first relationship and I was just tired of being emotional. It's almost as if I abandoned my connection to my emotions. I was tired of feeling weak.

For about six years, I operated with what I thought was logic. I prided myself on being intelligent, making smart decisions, and being more logical than emotional. One of my mentors at that time acknowledged what I accomplished but also thought I could accomplish more. He was a master influencer and to this day, I still haven't met anyone else with his degree of talent. His advice to me was to focus less on logic and more on emotions.

I resisted for a couple of years and then I finally took his advice. It was a game changer. My ability to influence shot through the roof, the way I operated internally was much more effective, and I got a lot more done. By leveraging the power of my feelings and those around me, I easily doubled my productivity. I also felt a lot better.

I had to find out why feelings and emotions were so powerful. I spent the next seven years studying how feelings influence your decisions and impact your quality of life.

All my experience and research led to a definitive conclusion: your fulfillment in life is directly proportional to your feelings, not your logic. You can think that you are fulfilled but it's not until you feel fulfilled that you truly experience it. Therefore, you can't think your way to fulfillment, you must feel it.

You may be tempted to skip this chapter. But out of all the subjects that I teach men, mastering your feelings is the most powerful.

The Power of Your Feelings

Everything you do is based on your feelings. You don't "think love" or "think hunger." You "feel love" or "feel hunger." You are a creature of emotions. You use logic to think and make decisions but the majority of your actions are based on your feelings. Even if you're a highly logical person, there's always underpinning feelings that direct your logic.

Most men use logic to justify their feelings. Let me repeat this. Most men use logic to justify their feelings!

That's why I mentioned in the introduction of this chapter that "I operated with what I thought was logic." It wasn't logic. It was my feelings masked by logic.

Your feelings are significantly more powerful than your thoughts. Imagine you have a single positive thought. It can lead to several different feelings such as joy or happiness or contentment. Now imagine having a single positive feeling like happiness. It can lead to dozens, if not hundreds of different thoughts. Your thoughts are more intense when feelings are added to them.

The Purpose of Feelings

Your feelings will either propel you towards your goals or hold you back. When you feel like you're on top of your game, it's like nothing can stop you. When you're in a rut, your feelings may even push you in the opposite direction of your goals. Maybe you have an underlying feeling of guilt, shame, or jealousy that's causing you to move away from where you want to be. There were moments when my wife and I were on the verge of splitting up and I was so angry at her, that I was ready to sabotage my own success. I was going to give her a real reason to criticize me. I didn't go through with it but I was close on a few occasions.

The purpose of your feelings is to get you to move. The word emotion is derived from the Latin word "motus" meaning motion. A thought can only get you to move so much. But a feeling can get you moving quick and hard. A feeling can enable you to endure the toughest situations and overcome your biggest barriers. Your thoughts are the sparks but your feelings are the fuel for your fire.

How Feelings Work

Your "feelings," are felt throughout your body. If you feel angry, the skin on your face will get flush, and you'll clench your fists. That's why it's so easy to respond by punching someone who makes you angry. It's your body's natural response to a threat. When you have a deep feeling of love for someone, you feel a warmth in your chest area. When you're hungry, you can feel your gut almost twisted.

A feeling is your body's way of telling you that you need to act. If you're feeling happy, continue to do what you're doing. If you're feeling afraid, then you need to move away from or overcome whatever is making you feel that way. Almost all of our human emotions originate from many millenniums ago. A hundred thousand years ago, humans had to fear being eaten by animals, starvation and sleeping in extreme weather conditions without proper shelter. Humans, for the most part, don't live that way anymore but we still carry these feelings and triggers. For example, your feelings can trick you into believing that your mother-in-law is a threat. You may hate listening to her insults, but is she truly a threat to you? Your feelings may tell you that she is.

Feelings are tricky. Let's say you're walking along and you stub your toe on a book laying on the floor. A signal from your toe travels to your brain. Your brain registers a feeling of pain. You look down and see the book on the ground and that tells your brain that your kid was sloppy. You then register a feeling of anger. You tell yourself that you're going to straighten your kid out. You call out for him and he ignores you. You then get even angrier. You shout his name even louder and he still ignores you. You stomp over to where he's watching tv, totally ignoring you. You begin to lecture him. You bring up everything he's done in the past and how he needs to get his act together or you're going to kick his ass out of the house. After eleven minutes of listening to you yell, he tells you that it's not his book. You walk back and realize that it's your book.

Your thoughts and feelings are in a constant cycle. One fuels the other and they create momentum. The example about stubbing your toe shows you how easily thoughts and feelings can escalate because they build on each other. It's very easy to have a single thought or feeling that turns into a cascade. The solution is to pause for a moment (or as long as you need) to properly appraise your feelings before you respond. Studies show that a feeling can easily pass in sixty to ninety seconds if it's not fueled.

Triggers

You are a walking talking bomb. All it takes is being exposed to certain feelings, and you are triggered. Your mother-in-law walks into the room and you feel angry; your wife tells you that you're not spending enough time with the family and you feel guilty; you show up late to a meeting and you feel embarrassed. Most of the feelings you live with today have been conditioned over time by a trigger. You've learned to feel this way based on past experiences.

The past conditioning from triggers creates two challenges. The first is that it's easier for you to be triggered if you've already been triggered in the past. Your brain has already made the neural connections, which means it's easier to feel that way the second time and then the third time and so forth.

The second is that by living with the same feelings, you are living in the past, not the present. If you automatically have a feeling towards an event today based on yesterday's feeling, then you're living in yesterday. You may not realize it but most of your feelings are conditioned based on what you have experienced vs. what you are experiencing now. It took my wife and I a while to break through our resentment because we had conditioned ourselves to feel the past, even though each day was new.

Your emotions can be conditioned in two different ways. The first is causation. You are exposed to stimuli (for example, your lawyer) and you feel a certain way (frustrated!). Your brain directly connects your lawyer to frustration.

The second conditioner is correlation, which is more of a general association. Your lawyer is in your office when you receive a phone call that someone in your family got into an accident. Next time you meet with your lawyer, you associate your lawyer with the feeling of sadness. Your lawyer had nothing to do with you feeling sad, but he was present when you heard the bad news and had those deep feelings. You can see how triggers can easily be created and how the majority of them are inaccurate and outdated.

Men and Feelings

How you deal with your feelings is based on your genetics as well as how you grew up. If your parents didn't show their feelings much, you're less likely to as well. But the genetic component has just as great an impact.

There are many stereotypes about men. The general public believes that men aren't creatures of feelings. The media and certain interest groups make men out to be cold as stone. Some psychologists hypothesize that men evolved to not show certain feelings that can demonstrate weakness. Weakness meant less food, less sex and less chances of passing your genes on. We've evolved to deal with our feelings in distinct ways.

Times have radically changed but our genetics have not. There are studies that show that men express and read facial expressions differently than women. Men may show a poker face with less emotion so that those around him don't sense his feelings which could be his weakness. On the flip side, aggressive criminals have been shown to have higher levels of testosterone based on their genetics. Men have genetic elements that impact their feelings and how they deal with them, just like women do. For example, women on average are more sensitive or emotional during particular periods of their menstrual cycle.

The cliche that men aren't emotional is completely false. Studies show that males are just as emotional as females but the male brain tends to switch over to problem-solving or decision making sooner or more predominantly than females. That's why when your wife tells you that she has a problem, you immediately want to fix it. Whereas she just wants to be heard and for you to listen. Men do feel, they just tend to want to get through the feelings faster and tackle the issue.

A second perception is that emotional men are weak. They are far from weak. Your feelings give you power. They are one of the three ways of experiencing life.

Remember, you experience life through thoughts, feelings and energy. Feelings are the most intense and satisfying. By learning how to leverage them, you can magnify your influence, impact, results and fulfillment. I get emotional and sometimes cry. I don't see it as a weakness and I don't hold it back. I don't get very emotional when I'm sad, stressed or angry. I get more emotional when I see a person succeed; when they've overcome their biggest challenges and demons to become complete. I'm guaranteed to shed a few tears in each episode of America's Got Talent.

A third perception is that men need to be more vulnerable. But men don't need to be more vulnerable, they just need to be more aware of their feelings and learn how to leverage them. They also need to understand the impact of their feelings on others. Your wife, kids, employees and everyone else around you absorb your feelings.

My dad was a very stoic man which gave my brother and I a feeling of safety and even admiration. My dad was tough and I knew that as long as he was around, nothing would hurt us. But when he drank too much, he lost his stoic presence. He became overly emotional and that was when we were afraid because we knew he couldn't hold it together, whether it was his anger, sadness or frustration. His vulnerability created fear within us.

When he didn't drink and he did show his emotions, it was amazing. He was one of the most emotional men I knew. He taught me that it's okay to be a man and that showing emotions is "manly." When our son was born and my dad was holding him, I saw tears in his eyes. Right now, just having that image in my mind now chokes me up.

Different Levels of Feelings

The more you understand the different levels of feelings, the more equipped you will be to master them. Based on the work of Oatley and Jenkins in *Understanding Emotions*, there are several types of feelings. If you're looking to change how you feel, then identify which of these levels you need to address:

- **Emotions** – which are short-lived from seconds to minutes and arise from interacting with stimuli in your environment. e.g. The school calls and tells you that your daughter broke her arm. You immediately feel concerned.
- **Moods** – which typically last a few minutes to a few days and are more of a state of mind. e.g. Your dog dies and you're sad for a few days.
- **Personality** – which is your baseline for your feelings and lasts months or years. These are your natural feelings that you feel on a daily basis. e.g. Some people are happier than others because that's part of their personality.
- **Culture** – which has the longest duration. If you compare the Japanese culture to the Jamaican culture, there's a stark difference. Emotions aren't widely shown in the Japanese culture whereas Jamaicans are boisterous.
- **Body Homeostasis** – which is your body's state in terms of health and wellness. When you eat healthier and take care of your body, you're more likely to have healthier feelings. The reverse is true as well. e.g. You have a stomach ache that throws off your whole day.

Feelings Are Energy

Feelings have a number of functions. The primary function is to get you to move. But there's also a secondary function of transferring information and energy to others. When you feel a certain way, others around can absorb your feelings. Their brain receives that information consciously and unconsciously so they know how to respond to you.

Psychologists believe that the ability to pick up on a person's feelings was an evolutionary advantage. For example, if I know you're angry and want to attack me, I have a better chance of surviving if I can pick up on those signals early and run.

Who is your favorite person to hang out with? Whoever it is probably makes you feel better in some way. You absorb their energy. Your feelings carry information and energy and you can use both to communicate and influence others.

Feelings and Performance

Your level of feelings determines your level of performance. Studies from Stanford showed that the degree that a person's feelings were involved in their decisions directly impacted their results. The more feelings involved in your goals, the more likely you will be to remain committed, persistent and passionate about that goal.

Get pumped up for your goals. It helps. When my son was younger, he would watch me work out and say, "Go daddy go!" I visualize him saying that and there's no way I can let him down by not completing the set. It works every time.

Spock from *Star Trek* is a perfect example of how lacking feelings can impact your overall judgment. Spock was half human but had trouble making decisions relating to other humans because he would only use logic. Studies show that people who score high on IQ tests may still have trouble with judgment, wisdom, and overall life skills if they aren't able to properly assess their feelings and the feelings of others. Additional studies have shown that people who have suffered from brain damage to the areas where feelings are processed have trouble performing at the same level. Feelings are an essential element for optimal decisions and performance.

Be the Master, not the Slave

To master your external world, you must first master your feelings. You can be the slave to your feelings or be the man who commands his feelings. If you think of your feelings as a weakness, they become a weakness. If you think of them as a strength, they become a strength. By understanding and mastering the principles behind feelings, you are in control of yourself. You won't fall victim to your circumstances. Whatever comes your way, you know that you'll be able to come out of the situation even stronger. You'll also live a more joyful, fulfilling life.

A man who embraces his feelings is complete. Feelings are natural. It's okay to feel whatever feeling you have inside of you whether it's anger, sadness, guilt or any other feeling. It's not the feeling itself but your response to the feeling that counts. The secret is to feel that feeling and if it's not empowering you, let it pass and let it pass quickly. If it is empowering you, fuel that feeling even more.

Your heart is elemental to mastering your feelings. Your heart sends more information to your brain than your brain does to your heart. Studies show that there may be twice as many neural connections going from the heart to the brain than the brain to the heart. You should embrace your heart, not ignore it.

For simple techniques to master your feelings, go to www.completemanbook.com/resources.

Summary Action Items

1. Be aware of the feelings by being in tune with your body.

2. Be aware of the triggers that cause you to feel a certain way. Learn to buffer those triggers.

3. Determine which level of feelings you need to work on: emotions, mood, personality, culture or body homeostasis.

4. Use the information and energy in feelings to influence yourself and others.

5. Put more feeling into your decisions and execution. You'll perform better.

Go to www.completemanbook.com/resources for basic techniques to master your feelings.

CHAPTER TWENTY

Life Energy

"Everything is energy and that's all there is to it. Match the frequency of the reality you want and you cannot help but get that reality. It can be no other way."

-Albert Einstein

"Purdeep, I wish I had more time," Brad told me in our first coaching sessions. He was a very successful entrepreneur who owned three different businesses. All three of his businesses were doing well but not great by his standards. He wanted to double his revenues in the next two to three years for each of his businesses which would require a significant amount of work and commitment.

After a few weeks, I realized that there wasn't much I could help him with on the business side. He was a pro and knew his industries and competitors well. He had an MBA from Harvard. I was learning a few things myself from him about his industry.

"Brad, there's not much I can do for you on the strategy side. Why do you feel like I can help you?" I asked.

He said, "I need you to help me get more time."

I was confused. Now in his mid-forties, Brad had a wife and three teenage kids. He was a very good father and made sure that he was there for his kids. He had plenty of money and he seemed to have time for doing the things he enjoyed.

But it wasn't more time Brad was looking for, it was more energy. He needed more energy so that he could get more done in the time he had in his business. He also needed more energy to spend quality time with his family. Although he was physically present with them, he didn't have the level of energy he wanted to be fully engaged. In many ways, he was doing all the right things and still not getting the completeness that he wanted.

Our focus, then, was to create more energy in his life. Brad didn't hesitate and went full force. Within a month, he felt like he doubled his productivity. He came to the conclusion that he could sell one of his businesses, grow the other two, make more money, and spend even more time with his family. Within a year, Brad told me, "I'm happier than I've been in a very long time."

Alignment

You can do all the right activities in life and still not get what you want. But it's not easy to explain why this happens. All I can say is that there is more to how you live your life than you think. There is an energy or forms of energy that, when you align with them, things just fall into place. If there is a part of your life that isn't going well even though you're trying as hard as you can and doing everything you believe you can to make it happen, it's time to reevaluate your state of energy.

It may be difficult for you to believe that there is more to this world that you can see, and that energy can change your life. Even now, I get frustrated at times and tell myself, "to hell with this energy crap, it doesn't work." Almost every time I do that, I get a sign that convinces me otherwise.

There is energy that you are drawn to and there is energy that you are repelled by. The universe gives you back the same energy you put out. If you're a pessimist, you'll receive a pessimist's life with few options. If you're an optimist, you'll be presented with opportunities at every corner. It's one thing to think like an optimist, but are you radiating that same energy? You can try to think positive and still have a negative vibe. You cannot fool the universe.

Focus on the energy you are transmitting. What you're putting out is what you're getting back. Sheer will, brute strength, and persistence to get things done only works for so long. You exert more energy than you need to. Eventually it feels like you're pushing a wheelbarrow with a flat tire and filled with boulders up a hill. Your life should feel like a challenge, not a struggle.

Science of Energy

Einstein based his work on formulas and evidence, not just hunches. As a scientist, even he knew that energy was the key to life. His famous formula $E = MC^2$ represents the basis of energy and the relationship between energy and matter. He shows that energy and matter are different forms of the same thing.

This means that your physical reality is made of energy that presents itself as matter because it's travelling at less than the speed of light. In simple terms, everything in your life is energy, including you.

Each thought and feeling you produce is a form of energy with a frequency that aligns with similar frequencies. Happy people will gravitate towards happy people. Sad people will gravitate towards other sad people. By thinking that you have wealth, you can create wealth. By thinking that you have good health, you can create good health. Your thoughts have the power to change your reality.

I would take this a step further and include feelings as well as thoughts. Your feelings are even more powerful. If there's something you want and you truly feel like it's already happened, you will eventually have it. I've used this approach since I was in high school and it's worked.

If you ask some physicists for their definition of energy, they will respond that "energy equals possibility." You are living in a realm of infinite possibility because you are surrounded by energy. Energy moves in and out of forms from pure energy to pure matter and when you learn to tap into it, you truly become the complete and mindful alpha male who creates your own destiny.

Your Most Important Resource

You can have the time to do something but still not have the life energy to enjoy it or get the most out of it. Every cell in your body operates on energy. In fact, you have energy units in your cells called mitochondria that are like little plants producing energy for your cells. If your mitochondria don't operate effectively to produce enough energy, your cells don't work properly.

Stop and think about this for a second. You have trillions of cells in your body that help you move, regenerate, think, feel and enjoy life. Every single one of them operates on energy. You are literally walking-talking energy.

People mainly use chemical, electrical, and mechanical energy. These are easy to identify: the food we eat turns into calories; our cells use chemical and electrical energy to communicate; our cells move which is mechanical energy. But there is another type of energy that scientists are trying to measure when it comes to human beings.

Electromagnetic energy exists on a spectrum that ranges from light to radio waves. Humans have the ability to create and tap into electromagnetic energy. Studies on subjects in meditative states show that it is possible to produce electromagnetic energy. Although the science is not conclusive at this point, it suggests that humans have the capacity to tap into a higher-level energy that we don't normally use.

Ancient teachers used this energy to heal, teach, and connect with others. Science is finally catching up and showing many of these teachings to be true. If you're relying on traditional forms of energy, you're going to get traditional results. If you tap into a higher-level source, you'll get higher-level results.

Focus Your Energy

Focus is your best tool for engaging and deploying energy. Arnold Schwarzenegger mentioned two things that allowed him to win Mr. Olympia seven times: discipline and focus. When he would work out, he put himself in a meditative state and focused all his energy so he felt like he was almost inside his muscles.

Directing your energy into a few areas may be a challenge for you. You're told that you should be able to balance being a businessman, father, husband, athlete, leader, and hero all at once. But you have to choose how much energy you want to put into each area. Your family may require more of your energy, especially if you have young kids. Your business may require more if you're just starting out or if there's a downturn. By effectively prioritizing and focusing your energy, you'll be better off in the long-run.

Don't fall into the trap of trying to be the best at everything all at once. The Complete Man knows how to flow in and out of different areas of his life like water. Sometimes you have to force yourself through the resistance in your life but most of the time you should be flowing through it or around it.

Present Moment

You need maximum energy and power in the present moment for

the task that is right in front of you. But you may be spending half of your time thinking about the past or future. Studies show that a person's thoughts are adrift up to 47% of the time. This means that you're constantly thinking about and diverting your energy to something you have zero impact on.

Right now, can you hit a baseball yesterday? Can you hit a baseball tomorrow? No, because the past and the future do not exist in this moment. The only place they exist is in your head. You can't change the past, and the only way you can influence the future is by what you do now.

Be intentional with your thoughts and energy. Think about the future when you need to think about the future. It could be during brainstorming sessions, daydreaming, goal-setting sessions or strategic sessions. Maybe you need to think about the past to learn something that will benefit you now or later. Use both past and future to your advantage.

Meditation

Meditation is one experience in which you should focus your absolute attention on your future. This is where your thoughts turn into pure energy and shift your future toward the one you want. You're using your brain to project your thoughts in the form of an energy at a specific frequency into the universe. The universe responds to these frequencies of thoughts by altering your future reality to align with your thoughts.

Your brain operates in multiple frequencies which are shown here:

- **Beta (14-30 Hz)** – Associated with alertness, increased concentration, problem solving and improving memory.
- **Alpha (8-13 Hz)** – Associated with relaxation, increasing positivity and decreasing stress.

- **Theta (4-8 Hz)** – Associated with REM sleep, reduced anxiety and relaxation. Theta brainwaves are the most common for those in a meditative or creative state. The easiest way to reach the theta state in meditation is to meditate immediately after you wake up in the morning and before you go to bed. During those periods, your brain is naturally in that state anyways.
- **Delta (1-4 Hz)** – Associated with deep sleep and relaxation.
- **Gamma (30-100 Hz)** – Associated with information processing and performance. Gamma brain waves are also associated with higher levels of meditation by monks and experienced meditators and associated with the feeling of "bliss."

Meditative or meditative-like states range from Alpha to Gamma brain waves. The calmer your conscious brain is, the greater your ability to tap into electromagnetic energy and project that into the universe.

Masculine/Feminine

Masculine and feminine energies are extreme opposites. When you are in your masculine energy, the world responds differently than when you are in your feminine. For example, if you're in a highly driven masculine state and focused on achieving the task at hand, you'll get a different reaction from people and your environment than you would if you were in a nurturing and connecting feminine state.

Again, you have both masculine and feminine energy within you. Think of these energies as tools in your toolbelt. For each job or task, you require different tools. You wouldn't use the same tool for every task. That would be like using a hammer to drill in a screw which wouldn't be so effective. The more versatile you are with your masculine and feminine energy, the more complete you will be as a man and the more energy you will have.

Frequency of Emotions

Emotions like sadness and anger have lower frequencies which are associated more with material objects. Higher emotions like love and joy are associated with pure energy.

The higher the frequency, the closer you are to pure energy. This means that when you are in lower level emotions like frustration, it's much harder to make events happen because you are trying to use matter to affect matter. It can work, but it takes effort and time. When you're in a higher emotional state, you're able to use energy to shift matter, which is easier and faster. When I really want to get things done fast, I meditate on it and elevate to a higher emotional state.

Converting Energy

A law of thermodynamics says that energy cannot be created or destroyed, but it can be converted from one form into another. You can convert your disempowering emotions into empowering emotions. Fear and anger are two emotions that can be powerful if converted and directed into an empowering form.

I know that some of my best workouts happen when I have a little anger in me. I push those weights extra hard. Empowering emotions like passion can also be converted into negative emotions. Have you had a moment when you were excited to attend an event but you got stuck in traffic? That excitement turned into frustration and even anger. That's why road rage happens. People's emotions convert to disempowering forms of energy.

Instead, practice positive energy conversion. There are advanced techniques I use with men to get them to shift from one energy to another. It works by shifting one emotion to another like sad to happy or angry to excited. Once they've mastered this technique, they are so in-tune with their energy that they can manually shift themselves from angry to happy in an instant. After some practice it becomes fun.

Next time your wife upsets you, imagine being happy about it. How much better would that feel? What would her response be like? You'll end up with a different outcome. Be playful with your emotions and energy. Approach it with curiosity and imagination.

Negative Energy

Every single stimulus your brain is exposed to carries a form of energy, from people to the media. Stay away from negativity as much as you can because your brain and body are absorbing it. Have you had the experience of being in a room when a person walks in and you have an immediate negative reaction to that person? They haven't said or done a single thing, but you can feel their negative energy. This is what I'm talking about.

You may not feel the energy but it's always there. Animals, like dogs, are able to pick up on negative energy. My dog, Rain, is a 135-pound South African Mastiff. She's a trained guard dog but she is also the most loving dog I've ever had. I know that when I'm away she'll protect my wife and kids. She's trained to keep people out of our yard and when you're on the outside of the fence, she will not let you in. However, once I let you in, she smothers you with love.

When my dad's older brother came to visit for the first time, she went right after him. I've never seen her do that before. My uncle had long harbored resentment and jealousy towards my dad and our family. You would have no clue about that upon meeting my uncle, but my dog knew what kind of man he was based on his energy. Stay away from negative energy, period!

Always be conscious of your own energy. Are you projecting positive or negative energy onto others and into the universe? Every thought, feeling and action you perform projects energy. The more conscious you are of this, the faster your life will change.

Summary Action Items

1. Be conscious of aligning your thoughts, emotions, energy and actions. The more aligned they are, the more powerful you become.

2. Prioritize and allocate your energy appropriately. It's your most important resource.

3. Focus your energy and avoid diluting it by constantly thinking about the past, future or multitasking.

4. Be in the present moment.

5. Meditate or use meditative-like states to project your thoughts and create your future.

6. Be versatile with your masculine and feminine energies.

7. Keep your frequency high with empowering emotions like joy, love and peace.

8. Convert disempowering energy into empowering energy. Energy is easily converted.

9. Stay away from negative energy.

10. Be conscious of the energy you are projecting onto others and into the universe.

CHAPTER TWENTY-ONE

Work-Life Balance

"To go beyond is as wrong as to fall short."

-Confucius

"I had a rough day at work today" my wife said after she came home from a 12-hour shift at the hospital. Every day is tough for her, dealing with patients dying from cancer. Some are in their 70's, others in their early 20's. I have no clue how she handles it. But I know that her smile lights up her patients and that's what counts the most.

One particular patient got to Ruby that day. He was a successful man in his sixties who was diagnosed with cancer but had a good chance of surviving. Most of the patients share their life story with my wife and he did as well. I think Ruby connected with him because he spoke about his daughter and how he didn't spend much time with her when she grew up because he was busy with his career. Ruby related to his story because when her father remarried and had another family, she didn't see him much after that.

This patient shared his personal belief about his situation with Ruby and what he said shocked her. It shocked me as well. Typically, when people face cancer, they are focused on the challenges it brings. Even though many of them are optimistic, cancer is still a very scary thought. This gentleman was different.

He said that his cancer was a blessing because it forced him to slow down. Now, he is forced to see what's most important in life, which is being with his daughter. He's going to take as much time as he can to create memorable moments with her.

At least he realized this before it was too late. Some men don't.

Balance Is Inevitable

Our planet is a self-balancing system. The wind flows from high pressure areas to low pressure areas. Electricity flows from one electrode to another to balance the charge. When an animal species overpopulates a region, the food sources of that species diminish and the population eventually rebalances.

Your body temperature is constantly rebalancing, along with your respiratory rate and your blood pressure. If your blood pressure is too high, you may get headaches or other symptoms. If your temperature is too high, you get dehydrated and your organs shut down. If you're walking and you lose your balance, you fall. Balance and re-balancing is a principle of the world.

Yet people spend more time working than enjoying life, more time complaining than expressing gratitude, and more time dealing with political discord than helping those in need. For thousands of years, men have ruled the world and suppressed women. Now the pendulum has swung the other way and men are feeling somewhat powerless. We're seeing the rebalancing of the pendulum with men stepping into power but in a more mindful way rather than controlling.

Your Balance

One small action can shift your balance significantly. You had sex with your wife and one sperm got through and impregnated her.

Now you have a child that takes up a lot of your time, energy, and even money. On the opposite side, you may spend every evening and weekend working, only to see a slight upturn in your career.

There is no perfect balance but a continuous act of balancing. It's the art of the teeter totter. You're up or you're down. When you find perfect balance in the middle, it's a great feeling for a moment. Then you realize that you've shifted and you're on your way up or down again. It's no fun to be way heavier than the other kid and be stuck at the bottom. And it's no fun to be as light as a feather and be stuck at the top. After a while, you realize that the goal isn't to be perfectly balanced but to enjoy the act of trying.

Do you feel like you have a healthy balance in your life? Do you have just as much free time to enjoy life as you do to work? Do you feel that your priorities are balanced? Do you have the freedom to enjoy the money that you have? Do you have the money to enjoy life the way you want to? If your wife and kids were asked whether your priorities are balanced, what would they say?

"You have to hustle and grind until you make it" or "I'll sleep when I'm dead." What garbage. The guys who pitch this are the same men who have unhealthy relationships with their wife and kids, or are suffering from high blood pressure from constant stress. At one time I was enamored by athletes or famous actors based on their accomplishments and lifestyles. With a closer look, and seeing them divorce their fifth wife for their new mistress, I knew that wasn't the life I wanted.

Is work-life balance achievable? I believe it is but not 100% of the time. Just like the teeter totter, there will also be times when you're at the top and times at the bottom when you have to work harder than normal and you have less time and energy for your family. Don't fall for either of these illusions. Two days before my dad passed away, he was jokingly saying that my mom would die first because she was constantly stressed. Ironically, he died alone while he was working.

Here's the question: "Is your life making you happy?" In addition, "Is your life making your family happy?"

An ancient philosopher declared that when we cross paths with a rich man, our tendency is to ask, "But is he happy?" Rarely do we encounter a really happy man and then ask, "But is he rich?"

If you're chasing a magic carrot, you may be like that donkey that never catches it. That carrot is just stringing inches from your face and you can't seem to get it no matter what you do. Days, weeks, months, and years can be spent trying to catch that same damn carrot.

What's the carrot that you're chasing?

Recalibrating

Find your point of balance and use that as your reference point. That way you know where you stand. Your balance point is where you feel the happiest. It's your internal compass. If you don't know where the balance point is, you may not know that you're completely off track until it's too late. If you're off your balance point, it should be by choice.

If you've lived your entire life out of balance so you don't know where your balance point is, it's time to explore and find out. You have to push yourself to do that. If you're a workaholic, you may have to force yourself to take more time off. Think of this as a fun exercise. You need to recalibrate yourself periodically and consistently.

Effort vs Progress

Effort and progress aren't the same thing. If you're giving it everything you have and you're not seeing progress, you know you need to change your approach.

I've had to change my approach over and over again. I do it until I see the progress that I'm looking for. Only then do I put in more effort to accelerate my results. I've watched men working tirelessly on their business or career with little or no progress. Yet something is telling them that they need to work even harder to get results. But it's not the effort that matters at this point, it's the approach.

When you take on a project or task, do it with complete intensity. I'm often offered potential partnerships or pitched new business ideas. Unless I'm completely and utterly enthusiastic, I will not even consider it. When I'm enthusiastic, I'm committed and when I'm committed, I'm intense and intentional. With intensity and intentionality comes productivity and progress.

All around the world, there's a fixation on work hours. Working longer is equated to success. But the opposite is true. The number of hours you work doesn't equate to your success or quality of life. The most successful men I know work smart. They work hard because it's a choice for them, not because they think they have to.

Sprints

To get more done, sometimes you have to slow down. The law of diminishing returns describes a point beyond which the energy invested brings diminishing returns. Basically, you get less "bang for your buck" after a certain point. Working 70 hours a week won't give you that much more productivity than working 55 hours a week. You can achieve the same amount in less time by being more intentional and productive.

You become more intentional and productive by slowing down or taking breaks to regain your physical, emotional and mental capacity. Boxers don't fight 12 rounds without a break. Instead they fight in rounds with breaks in between. The 12 rounds can be called sprints; sprints are periods of time where you work intensely hard and then take breaks to revive.

Schedule sprints to suit your lifestyle. You can work hard for five days and then take the weekend off. You can work two weeks in a row and take a week or two away. You can work six months straight and take six months off. Find what works for you. My sprints are based on working five days and taking weekends off.

When you take your breaks, remove yourself from work completely. Allow your mind and body to experience the joys of life. Even if you don't feel like you haven't accomplished enough, be disciplined about taking your breaks. Avoid making excuses to have to do the work "right now." Most of the time, it doesn't need to be done "right now."

Burnout

Burnout affects more men each year. You might be on the verge of burnout yourself. In my executive career, I worked with a very capable young man who was smart as a whip. He had a ton of potential, but he was told by his doctor that he had to minimize his stress.

Several years before I met him, he had a good career, had a young family and he was refereeing hockey. His goal was to become a referee in the National Hockey League, which he was only steps away from attaining. He told me he was spending more time working, providing for his family, and trying to become a referee than he was resting.

Then he had a stroke. He was only in his thirties and as a

result, he lost his dream of becoming an NHL referee. He was also limited in his career progression because more stress would mean greater risk to his health.

Burnout has a price. You may be able to repay it in a short period of time, or the price may be too high to ever repay. Many marriages, relationships, dreams, and even lives have been lost from burnout. Is it really worth it?

Burnout = Energy Out > Energy In

Burnout occurs when your energy output is greater than the energy you take in. The energy can be caloric energy, mental energy, emotional energy or spiritual energy.

There are different types of burnout and the symptoms differ based on your own sensitivity. I spend hours and even days pouring everything I have into men who attend my workshops and by the time I'm done, I'm wiped out. My body is accustomed to hard physical labor so I can stand for hours without feeling physically exhausting. But my emotional energy is depleted and I need an emotional break. Some of my colleagues can only stand for a couple hours before they're physically exhausted. But emotionally they can go on for a longer period of time.

Performance psychologists have categorized burnout into these areas:

- **Cognitive burnout** – Burnout of the mind e.g. spending all day in a brainstorming session and you just can't think straight after.
- **Physical burnout** – Burnout of the body e.g. spending a day on a gruesome hike and you collapse when you get home.

- **Behavioral burnout** – Burnout of the activities involved. e.g. you spend weeks training for a competition and you just don't want to do the same training anymore.
- **Motivational burnout** – Burnout of motivation. e.g. you spend weeks training for a competition and you just don't want to compete anymore.

Burnout can also occur from prolonged stress, so be conscious of your triggers. Always be aware of how much energy you're burning and how much energy you're recharging yourself with.

The best way to avoid energy burnout is not to minimize the energy you expend but to maximize the energy that you take in and absorb. Maximizing energy involves taking breaks.

Shutting Off Work

How often do you think about work when you're with your family? Probably much too often. Let's face it, it's not easy to shut off work. There's an expectation in the modern world that you're supposed to be "on" 24/7. But there is a way to shut work off.

As much as I wanted to spend time with my family, I was having a difficult time doing it. I'd find myself playing with my kids and then drifting back into work. I knew there had to be a way I could train my brain to stay present. After using basic neuroscience principles and testing them on myself, I finally found the method. If you're having trouble shutting off work, here's what you need to do:

1. **Finish your task**– By finishing a task, you're telling your brain that you are done. By leaving it unfinished, you're telling your brain that you're not done and your brain will continue to think about it. Your brain continues to focus on unfinished tasks or problems until they are completed.

You may even have to create a mini task at the end of your workday just to check it off and tell your brain that you're done.

2. **Create a ritual** – A ritual tells your brain that you are entering a new situation. A new situation requires new thinking and a new approach. After a while, the ritual will automatically switch your brain into the new mode unconsciously. E.g. my ritual is taking a hot shower and immediately after, I'm in relax mode. No more work for me.

3. **Set a goal** – Have a goal for parts of your life outside of work. A goal gives your brain a target and remember that your brain is a goal-driven organ. The problem is that when you don't have goals outside of work, your brain is constantly thinking about the only goals it knows and those are most likely associated with your work. When I'm done with my work, my goal is to make my kids laugh for ten minutes.

4. **Switch your identity** – Your identity with your family should be different than your identity at work otherwise you're going to operate the same way and be stuck in work mode. Choose a new identity to be when you're with them. When I'm with my kids, I'm Disney Dad!

Summary Action Items

1. Balance your life because if you don't, something or someone else will force you to.

2. Find the balance that works for you. It's typically when you're the happiest.

3. Recalibrate yourself and your life at least once a year.

4. Evaluate whether your efforts are creating the progress you want. If not, change your approach.

5. Take business and life in sprints. Periods of working hard followed by breaks.

6. Avoid burning out by ensuring that you are recharging your energy more than you are expending it.

7. Use the methods in this chapter to shut work off so you can spend time enjoying your family and life.

CHAPTER TWENTY-TWO

Friends, Colleagues, Companions

"A great relationship is about appreciating the similarities and respecting the differences. "

-Unknown

During my early corporate career, I focused on being the most intelligent and hardest-working person in the room. I got along with everyone and had good working relationships. I did well, but not at the pace I wanted. I saw others moving up who were less qualified than me.

I was perplexed. Why was this happening? One of my mentors mentioned that I needed to "work" my relationships a little more. But I viewed that as sucking up and manipulating. I had gotten to where I was based on my performance. I had been working hard since I was nine years old. No one did me any favors. I wasn't going to be a kiss-ass no matter what. That wasn't me.

Sometime later, I came across a book that included a passage from Marcus Aurelius. For Marcus Aurelius, building and nurturing relationships was how wise men lived their lives. He strived to build relationships with his enemies even when they conspired to kill him. If a famous Roman emperor viewed all relationships this way, maybe I could as well.

I tried an experiment. Instead of focusing on tasks and getting the job done, I started to focus more on the relationships I had. Surprisingly, things started to happen a lot faster. I got promoted and I made more money. At the same time, I was deeper into my neuroscience and psychology studies which allowed me to take these relationship skills even further. It became natural to influence and move in the direction I wanted based on my connections with other people.

When I'm having exploratory calls with potential clients, I don't have to sell. I truly care about the men I work with and that comes across. The feedback I've received from clients is twofold: they've worked with other coaches and haven't seen the results they want. They connect with me and feel there's a genuine connection. I now base my work and my life on relationships regardless of how big or small.

Your Relationships Define You

The quality of your relationships defines the quality of your life. You're happier when you have better relationships, and studies also show a strong correlation between your relationships and your length of life.

The word "social" is defined as "needing companionship and best suited for living in communities." Biologists believe that some of the most influential factors in human evolution have come from the social environment. We have evolved into who we are based on our relationships with others. Our minds and bodies evolved based on how we interacted with each other for hundreds of thousands of years. If social relationships have impacted evolution to such a large degree, what impact do you think they have on your life?

Granted, it's tough to have good relationships with everyone. I have ongoing connections with many people who have hurt me in the past or I might not see eye-to-eye with. But I still care for them.

You never know where things can lead. I was at a client's office in the US and I struck up a conversation with one of his employees. I live in Canada on the opposite coast and it turned out this employee's brother lived right down the street from me. What are the chances of that? Nothing substantial came about from this coincidence but I did develop a stronger relationship with that employee based on a simple connection.

You don't have to be friends with everyone but you are a social being. You are in a relationship with everyone you come in contact with, even the guy who delivers your pizza. The relationship may be short-lived or lifelong, intense or superficial. You may benefit or you may not. But you are building relationships every day, everywhere with everyone you are in contact with.

How you perceive yourself is the most important element for being a Complete Man, but how others perceive you is also important. You can think of yourself as a hotshot but if others perceive you as an arrogant prick, you're going nowhere. If all the men out there perceived me as arrogant, I wouldn't have any clients since most of my business is based on referrals. In a social context and from a business perspective, your relationships define you.

Your Pride

Think of yourself as a lion, the leader of your pride. You may even have multiple prides. You can have your work pride, your family pride, your pride of friends and community pride. Define who is in your pride. Do you know each person well? Are you aware of what value they bring or what contribution they make? Does each person understand their own role and the role of others in the pride?

Every member of your pride contributes to the pride in some way. Those who do not contribute or bring value to the pride must be evaluated to see if they belong in your pride.

It sounds harsh but your duty as the leader, the mindful alpha male, is to ensure that your pride is strong. The strength of your pride is determined by the strength of the strongest members but also the weakness of the weakest members.

The duty of the alpha is to set the direction of your pride, to encourage and inspire each member and ensure that the pride is progressing towards the goals. Alphas can be viewed as being harsh and strict but true alphas are the complete opposite. They practice compassion and empathy with their members. They try to understand things from other's perspectives and put themselves in other's shoes. They understand that each person does the best they can with what they know. It's the alpha's job to ensure that the member understands how to step up and progress.

If a member is unable to move forward based on mental, physical or emotional limitations, then the alpha accommodates for their challenges. However, if the member is just plain lazy or unwilling, then the alpha must make the decision to limit the member's interactions with the group or remove them all together. Lead with love and compassion but also know that it doesn't solve everything. Choose your pride members wisely.

Choose Wisely

The people you associate with should accept you for who you are. They should also push you and support you in overcoming your challenges. Associating yourself with the wrong crowd can hold you back in many ways. Building relationships with the right people can greatly accelerate your growth and progress. Jim Rohn, an American motivational speaker and pioneer of personal development, said that you are the average sum of the five closest people you associate yourself with. Who are these five people in your life?

I look at three things when considering whether I will spend time with a person. The first is alignment in values. I have strong values and I live my life according to certain principles. I have no interest in people who lie, cheat or have bad intentions. I'm repelled by that energy.

My second consideration is interdependence. Can we share value in each other's lives? This doesn't mean financial value or exchange of goods. It's more about knowledge, experiences or even fun. There needs to be some value on both sides for the relationship to work long-term.

Finally, how will this person help me grow? Is there something he or she knows that I don't? Maybe they have different perspectives that I should be aware of or maybe they'll challenge my current thinking.

I love being around people who I learn from. I especially love people who challenge me because it means I get to see the world from a different perspective. Seeing things from the same angle over and over again gets boring. Being around people who agree with everything you say isn't the best strategy. That's like a bunch of cows following each other around the pasture.

Having criteria for your relationships doesn't mean presuming yourself to be better than others. It means that you are selective in where you place your energy and time. You don't need to ignore anyone. You may just have to limit your interactions with them.

How Do You Feel?

How do you know if you're associating with the right people? The best way of knowing is by awareness of how you feel about yourself. You can associate with people who pump you up with compliments, but how do you really feel when you're around them?

There was a short period of my life when I partied a lot and got to know some shady guys. I never got involved in drugs or anything like that, but these guys were deep into it. We constantly had hot girls around and got VIP treatment wherever we went. It was flattering to be surrounded by attractive women who had an interest in me. But after a while, I didn't feel good about myself. It just wasn't my crowd. They made me feel good, superficially, but I didn't feel good about myself. It just didn't feel right for me.

Do you have empowering feelings when you're with someone? Do you feel proud, happy, content, uplifted, joyful, ambitious, supported and inspired? These are just a few of the many feelings you can have around people who empower you. Your heart will tell you the truth. Sometimes your mind can deceive you but your heart doesn't.

I had a business relationship with a very successful and well-connected entrepreneur. He knew powerful individuals and celebrities around the world. I had open access to him as I was coaching him and his executives.

When I first met him, I was immediately turned off by him. I got the impression that he was all about himself so I didn't engage with him any further. I met him again several years later and this time he was adamant about getting my help. I agreed and worked with him for almost a year.

At first it was great. He connected me with many of the influential men in his circle. But after several months, he became very self-serving. He was trying to leverage my connections for his benefit.

I soon picked up on his strategy. He would lay the bait out for me so he could get what he wanted. Initially, I thought this was fair. It was a business arrangement and business includes trade-offs. I was telling myself, "What's the big deal. I'm benefiting from him. Just keep going. No one is getting hurt and we're both winning." But every interaction became a barter. You scratch my back and I'll scratch yours. Each conversation with him would make my gut wrench.

I told myself that the next time would be different, but it never was. He was always fishing for what he could get out of me. Eventually, I had enough and disengaged. The money I was making wasn't worth the feeling I got from interacting with him.

Wisdom Council

When you face tough decisions or face challenging situations with relationships or any other matter, it's good to have a council of wise people on your side. It's the group of people you go to for help to answer your tough questions. I call my own group of wise men and women my Wisdom Council.

Whenever I'm in a tough situation, I ask myself, "What would my Wisdom Council say?" I then go through each individual one by one to see things from their perspective. For those council members who are still alive, I may even call them up directly and get their insight. It sounds quirky but it's a great practice. You can change members based on your situation in life or if you need new perspectives. I'm constantly adding new members and modifying my council.

Respect

You don't have to agree with me or even like me but hopefully you can respect me as a human being. That's the attitude we need more of in the world. There is far too much hate and division than what healthy nations should have.

There's nothing wrong with people having different beliefs or conflicting values. There's never been a time in history where everyone has gotten along perfectly. But of course, we can do better by respecting each other. This is part of being a mindful alpha male. The moment we lose respect for a person as a human being, the differences turn into bitterness and resentment.

There are three levels of respect:

- **Respect for beings** – The basic respect for all living beings. We share this world in a collaborative ecosystem.
- **Respect as a human** – The basic respect for a person. A person is a living, breathing human being who has a soul and feelings. They may not be perfect but they are living. Every person does the best they can based on their circumstances.
- **Respect based on roles** – The respect you have for the role they play in your life. Your father has a role, your wife has a role and your colleagues have a role. Everyone in your life has a role they play.

If someone in your life isn't living up to your expectations, you don't have to respect them based on their role, but at least respect them for being a human and a living being. If your employee screws up and you decide to fire him, that doesn't mean you need to disrespect him as a person. He may be a good person but just not the right fit for the role. By separating the role from the person, you may have a little more compassion and empathy.

Without respect, healthy relationships don't exist, and without healthy relationships, there is no society. Ancient philosophers described the people of Rome as "a mob." Mobs are prevalent in modern times as well. Daoism, a Chinese philosophy, states that when we lose our natural respect for each other, we look to justice to solve the problem. This would be our current equivalent of the legal and political system. When justice fails, we look towards rituals. This is blind faith, following practices just because it's the way they've always been done. We see that around the world today.

Love and Kindness

The natural cement of relationships is love and kindness. When in doubt, just love and be kind. You can't go wrong. Even if the other person doesn't reciprocate it, you still feel good about yourself. Love is the universal language. It's the one thing you can give over and over again without limits. It's the one thing that no one can stop you from giving. Every person wants to feel loved, even those who reject it. Some people just don't know how to accept love. They may have never felt it before and therefore it's foreign to them. It's important to give them love so they learn how to accept it.

When Jack Canfield, co-author of the *Chicken Soup for the Soul* series, endorsed my last book, *Super Fans*, he shared a profound story. He was at an airport when there was an announcement that his flight would be delayed. It was a very small airport and he was afraid that food would run out so he bought some food for himself.

As he returned to the gate, he saw that another man had also bought some food. But this man was giving it away to other people. Jack felt horrible and he said that day taught him a big lesson. From that point forward he asks himself, "What would love do in this situation?" I ask myself this question all the time now and it keeps me out of a lot of trouble. You can't go wrong by giving too much love or kindness.

Just a note of coincidence. As I was writing the last sentence in this chapter, I received a call from my wife. She was at the hospital with my daughter who almost drowned in her friend's pool. Luckily my wife was there and having a medical background she was on top of the situation. My initial reaction was, "How could this happen? Weren't the parents being careful? Why wasn't she wearing a life jacket?" I was flooded with anger!

Then I reminded myself to practice love and kindness. This allowed me to approach the situation from a much calmer and rational perspective. Thankfully, my daughter is fine.

Summary Action Items

1. Evaluate the quality of your relationships. Remember that they define you.

2. Take inventory of your prides and the members of your pride. Do you have the right members in your prides?

3. Associate with people who you feel good being around.

4. Create a wisdom council to give you guidance.

5. Give basic respect to everyone for being human.

6. Lead with love and kindness.

CHAPTER TWENTY-THREE

The Meaning of Life

"The meaning of life is that it is to be lived."
-Bruce Lee

I walked into the family room after I came back from school and saw my dad sitting on the floor against the couch.

"Hi dad," I said as I walked past him to go upstairs. Barely looking at me, he said, "Hello, son" in Punjabi. It was strange for him to be sitting like that doing nothing. If he was going to rest, he would usually nap or watch television. Otherwise he was always doing something around the house.

I went upstairs, put my bag away and walked into the TV room where my mom was watching a program. I don't remember how much time passed but my dad eventually came upstairs and sat on the ground next to us.

Without a word, he just started vomiting. His eyes rolled into the back of his head and blood came out of his mouth. Blood and a foamy vomit.

My mom started to panic and scream. She doesn't do well in high stress situations and sometimes even passes out. This time she kept it together enough to start shaking my dad and telling him to wake up. I ran to the phone and called 911. He eventually went completely unconscious with his body convulsing. The rest was a blur.

The ambulance came and took my dad to the hospital emergency room. When mom and I arrived, a doctor told us that he was stable but had significant damage to his stomach and intestines. They were pumping toxic chemicals out of his system.

The doctor asked us if we knew what he had ingested. My mom and I had no clue until the doctor mentioned that it was something very poisonous. The only poison we had at home was used to spray the orchard. It clicked for my mom, and she told the doctor what she thought it was. They did what they needed to in order to save his life.

As my dad regained consciousness, I remember standing next to his bed feeling completely confused. What happened? Was it an accident? What's going on? Had he tried to kill himself?

My dad was the tough guy, not someone who would do that. I didn't know what to say to him. I was just glad that he was alive. Later that day, my dad's personal doctor walked in. He was my dad's doctor since my dad immigrated from India, so he knew my dad well. He asked my dad a few questions and then said something that made my dad smile.

"You have reason to live. You have a beautiful wife and two beautiful sons. That's your reason."

I never once asked my dad why he did what he did but I knew. He felt like he didn't have a reason to live. I'm not sure why he felt that way, but he did.

What Is the Purpose of Life?

This question can be answered in two parts.

The first part concerns the universal meaning for everyone on this planet. As Bruce Lee put it, the meaning of life is to live it. Life is meant to be enjoyed, savored, embraced, and experienced to the fullest. If we overindulge in philosophy, we may forget to live our own life to the fullest. Even if your life doesn't seem to be going your way, there is always beauty to be found. Go out there and do what you want to do and live the way you want to live. You would not have been given life if you were not meant to enjoy it.

The single caveat is to be mindful of your actions. The Complete Man is a mindful man who does for others as much as he does for himself. His joy comes from the joy of others.

Experience life on your terms as long as you're not hurting anyone else. I dislike how some spiritual mentors make worldly desires out to be "evil." Yet they're taking in all the cash from donations, travelling the world, staying in nice hotels and being treated like royalty. Desires are natural and they are meant to be satisfied but they should be satisfied for reasons that make sense. Buy a big house if you want a place to entertain, for example. Don't buy it to impress your friends because that'll never give you true satisfaction. Be true to your own desire and not the desires of others.

The second element to the meaning of life concerns who you are as an individual, with your unique soul, energy, mind, body, and purpose. I cannot tell you what your unique and individual purpose is, and it would be absurd for me to even try.

Your unique meaning is connected to your life's purpose. Your purpose drives your passion which drives your priorities which ultimately leads to your progress. I call those the Four P's.

Your purpose doesn't have to be grandiose; it just has to mean something to you. You don't have to save the whales to have meaning. Raising healthy and happy children could be your meaning, or being an amazing husband; both of these are part of my meaning.

If you're looking for your purpose, give yourself some credit. Especially, don't feel like another man can do it better than you. In each of us, there is a small voice that tells you that you are not enough or that you are an imposter. That's just your mind playing tricks on you. Stand up and take control of your purpose. No one else is you or lives your life. Therefore, you are the best person for your purpose.

If you don't know what your purpose is, find it. Ken Keis, author of *The Quest For Purpose*, was a guest on my podcast and shared this great insight: "If you don't have a purpose, your purpose should be to find your purpose." To listen to the entire interview, go to *The Male Entrepreneur* podcast episode 98, "How To Find Your Life Purpose" at www.PurdeepSangha.com/podcast.

Finding your purpose should be taken seriously but not too seriously. Take time to think about it but don't let it stress you out. Your purpose is meant to drive you so you should be passionate and committed to it. A half-ass purpose will lead to less than half-ass results.

After working with countless men looking for a purpose that invigorates them, I have seen a common theme. The men who are most passionate about their purpose have one that is centered around others and not themselves. A purpose for yourself is limited because it's for just one person. A purpose for others can be infinite.

Passion

How alive do you feel? Do you jump out of bed eager to experience your day or are you dreading the events to come?

Worst of all is being in between, in the zone of indifference where you have no passion but life isn't that bad either. You're just doing the same things over and over again. You have little motivation to change.

My purpose is to help men experience complete victory. I'm so passionate about it that I get chills when I think about giving up. I couldn't, even if someone tried to force me. It's what gets me up in the morning and drives me through every challenge I have. My passion allows me to take the criticism from those who think my work is sexist and bash me. It's nothing compared to my level of passion.

But your purpose alone shouldn't drive your passion. There should be a passion for life in general. You live in a beautiful world with beautiful people. No movie, virtual reality or artificial intelligence can compare to breathing fresh air into your lungs as you feel the warmth of the sun and its beauty as it rises in the morning. Life itself is passion.

The Walking Dead isn't a TV series, it's reality for many men. They walk around like zombies with no passion or drive for life. Save being dead for when you're dead. Right now, you're alive so find some passion in it.

Experiences and Memories

A simple way to create more meaning is to be intentional with the experiences you create for yourself and others. Everything is an experience. You know that you're alive because you are experiencing life and you're doing it with all your thoughts, feelings, and energy as I've mentioned before.

Think of life as a series of experiences. Many of them will be random but many of them you can create. If you're going out for dinner with your wife, do something nice for her and go the extra mile. Maybe that's as simple as buying her some flowers. Who is that person in your life that does a little extra for you? Maybe it's your grandma who bakes you those amazing pies, or maybe it's your Aunt Mary who makes your favorite cookies. How do you feel when you're around that person? Pretty good, I'm sure. That person feels good about it too. Creating experiences for others is a selfless way to create more meaning.

Wonderful moments create wonderful memories. Memories are all that you have from experiences besides the trinkets you acquire, and the real value in trinkets is in the memories they spark in your mind. One day only memories will remain. Make those memories count. Try to make your experiences as memorable as possible, for you and especially for others.

Questions

The questions you ask yourself will determine your quality of life. Your mind is constantly asking and answering questions. Some of the questions are from the external environment but the vast majority are from inside your own mind. If your mind is asked a question, it will find an answer. Your mind is programmed to find an answer. If someone asks you why you're a failure, you will find a reason for it.

Ask yourself good questions. Instead of asking why you have a hard time expressing your feelings, for example, ask what you can do to express your feelings more openly. A slight shift in how you ask the question, can have a tremendous impact on the answer.

During a visit to Japan, I learned a great lesson from a Japanese executive. He said, "Any fool can solve a problem. The intelligent man solves the right problem." Ask empowering questions and you will get answers that empower you. Ask yourself disempowering questions and you will get answers that disempower you.

You have default questions that are the questions you ask yourself on a consistent basis. They are also the default questions you ask yourself when things go right or wrong.

Do you know what these questions are? Keep a journal of them and you'll eventually find a pattern. If your questions are empowering questions (e.g. "How can I learn from this?") that's great. If they are disempowering questions (e.g. "Why does this always happen to me?) then it's time to change them. By consciously asking new default questions, you will eventually override the old ones.

Try to align your default questions with the identity you have created for yourself. For example, if part of your identity is being a courageous leader, then the question could be something like "what would a courageous leader do in this situation?"

Value

Your meaning can also come from the value you bring to this world. It could be the value you bring to your relationship with your wife. It could be the value you bring to your business. Or it could be the value you bring to your relationships with your employees. Society operates on value. If an object or person doesn't bring value to an arrangement or relationship, it's eventually discarded.

A successful man can have his model wife walk out on him when his business goes bankrupt and he's left with no money. The value she saw in him was his money, not him. I've seen this happen. Money and material goods only provide so much value. Unless you're feeding the hungry and the poor, your main value comes from the relationships you have with the people around you. You don't have to spend a single dime or make tons of money to be valued. All you need to do is to genuinely make people feel good. This is the most priceless value you can have in life. No one can take that away from you.

Locus of Control

Meaning and control are closely correlated. If you feel like you've lost control of your life, it's easy to feel like you don't have meaning. If you've lost your job and are having difficulty finding employment, your sense of meaning may diminish.

Often men who lose their jobs or have underperforming businesses, lose a big portion of their meaning. Their center of control was their work and when they don't have that control anymore, they feel lost. I felt that way after I quit my executive career. For the first few months, I felt like I had no control. I felt like I had no control over the direction of my new business, my finances and even my sense of purpose.

Locus of control is the degree to which you believe that you have control over the situations and experiences that affect your life. If you feel like you are powerless to your circumstances, your locus of control will be low. If you feel that you can influence and direct your circumstances, you will have a higher locus of control. The greater your locus of control, the greater your chances of being able to direct the meaning in your life.

Optimists vs Pessimists

Optimism can also impact your sense of meaning and quality of life. Studies show that optimists are more successful and live longer than pessimists. It makes sense because optimists tend to have less stress than pessimists and they tend to have better relationships. No one enjoys being around a pessimist unless they are a pessimist themselves!

Studies also show that optimists see challenges and failures as situational. They see them as external and don't internalize them. Pessimists internalize challenges and failures and fester over them. It's the difference between "I lost my job so I need to upgrade my skills so I can get a better one" and "I lost my job because I'm not good enough. They found someone better to replace me." It's the same situation with different attitudes that create different meanings. Be an eternal optimist.

Changing Your Meaning

Can your meaning change throughout your life? Absolutely. Your meaning should be relevant to your life stage. Your meaning can change as you go through different life stages or life-changing events. When you got married, did your meaning change? I'm sure it did. When you had your first child, did your meaning change? Of course. When someone close to you passed away, did it impact your meaning? I'm sure it had an impact.

You don't have to stick with the same meaning your entire life because you're human and humans change and evolve. If you have the same meaning you did as a horny fifteen-year old, I'd be a little worried.

Challenges

There is no meaning without challenge. If it's too easy, it's not going to be meaningful enough. The more resistance you face, the more passionate you will be for your meaning. The games that the greatest athletes remember the most, aren't those where they easily beat the other team. They are the games where the other team made them work every inch for the win.

With greater resistance comes greater power, meaning, and growth. When you face your greatest challenges, reach down to the depths of your soul and you'll find the power you need to overcome them. In some ways, resistance is meaning.

Be vs Have

Your meaning will be much more powerful if it's based on "being" rather than "having." Having only lasts for so long before you get tired of it. There are only so many cars you can buy, watches you can wear and followers on social media you can have before it becomes old news. Instead, be the man you were meant to be. Be the complete version of you, be The Complete Man.

There is greatness inside you. A victor, a man who doesn't settle for mediocrity. A man who doesn't give up at the first sign of a challenge. A man who stands up as a role model and teaches other men how to live more meaningful lives. If each of us men mentored one other man or child, think of how much better we could make this world? This is how you can experience complete victory.

Summary Action Items

1. Enjoy your life to the fullest.

2. Find your particular meaning. Only you can live this meaning out because there's only one of you.

3. Live with passion.

4. Create amazing memories and experiences for yourself and others.

5. Ask yourself empowering questions rather than disempowering questions.

6. Add value to others and this world.

7. Have a high locus of control so you can create your meaning and life.

8. Be an eternal optimist.

9. Evolve your meaning to be relevant to where you are in life.

10. Welcome challenges as they add meaning to your life.

11. Rather than *getting and having* things, focus on *becoming and being* The Complete Man.

CHAPTER TWENTY-FOUR

Your Legacy

"The goal isn't to live forever; the goal is creating something that will."

-Chuck Palahniuk

I thought I would be okay when I approached the podium with my brother to give my father's eulogy, but I wasn't okay. I felt my throat tense up and my arms and hands started to quiver. A deep sadness went through my body and I wept as my brother put his hand on my back to console me. He too was doing his best to hold back his tears.

This was our dad, a man we loved. A man we learned so much from who is no longer here to guide us. He wouldn't be there to play with our kids. He wouldn't be around to teach our kids the lessons he learned throughout his life, or to teach them the history of India that he had experienced. We wouldn't see his big smile and deep laughter that just made us all want to smile and laugh. My brother and I would be on our own from now on.

I didn't write out a specific eulogy for my dad because I wanted it to be straight from the heart. That's who my dad was. He was a straight up man who wore his heart on his sleeve. I thought I should be the same way.

There were many things I wanted to say about my dad but I said what was most important. He was a man who loved his family and gave everything he had so we could have a happy life. He was a man who loved others with all his heart and all he wanted in return was to be loved himself. He knew he wasn't perfect, and that was the most beautiful part of him. He didn't expect others to be perfect because he knew he was flawed himself.

My dad is the driving force of my life's mission to help men achieve complete victory. If he hadn't been who he was – a great father and at times a not-so-great father – I wouldn't have the skills to help other men.

My dad was not The Complete Man and he didn't experience complete victory. I knew that something was missing for him and he was feeling incomplete. He's no longer here but his legacy is here.

Dad, I will always cherish you for who you were. I love you.

Each Day Counts

Legacy isn't about what happens after your death. It's about how you live while you're alive. The impact that you have today has a ripple effect throughout time. You can choose to go through life with no impact, little impact, or with a significant impact. You don't have to be Martin Luther King Jr. to have a legacy. Just be the best man you can be for the people around you.

"I will when I.......?" is the grim reaper of legacy. Why wait? What's holding you back? What can you do to magnify your impact today? There is no point in waiting. The man who acts now is the man who experiences victory. My dad had many aspirations of what would happen after he turned 65. He wanted to travel more, spend more time with his grandkids and go on family trips. He never saw those days because he died at sixty-four and a half. Don't let that be your story.

Focus on What's Most Important

My wife works with patients dying of cancer and not one of them has talked about wanting to have achieved more. They all want more time with the people they love. They want to spend a few more moments with family and friends. They want to experience the feeling of loving and being loved.

One of my wife's patients was a forty-year-old woman. She suffered from multiple types of cancers and eventually asked for assisted suicide because it was too painful for her. Ruby attended the procedure which was extremely difficult for her and she was heart-broken. She and her team remembered the same thing about this woman. She always had a smile on her face that made everyone else smile. I know that Ruby will remember her for as long as she lives.

Goals and achievement are important but if they're keeping you from enjoying your life – and from having a positive, lasting impact on your loved ones – it's time to set your priorities straight. Watch *The Family Man* with Gerard Butler. It's a powerful story which I won't ruin for you, but it's a must watch. Many men live as Gerard does in this story. Some have happy endings, others don't.

I have to give my dad credit. He was always there for us. We never felt like he wasn't around and we never felt like we weren't loved by him. We knew that he would be there for us whenever we needed him. He never held back his love; he always gave it openly even to strangers. Do the people around you feel the same way about you?

It's All About Love

People don't care what you do for them as much as they care about how you make them feel. When my dad passed, I spent several weeks with my mother. Men, who I had never met, showed up at our doorstep weeping. Each of them shared a story of how my dad went out of his way for them and made them feel special. It was strange watching grown men as old as my dad cry for him. I never knew that he made that impact on others.

The love and kindness you share with others is eternal. It is the most powerful connection you can create.

Levels of Impact

What you do on a daily basis has four levels of impact. Each of these levels is just as important as the others. All four are dependent on each other. The universe is bound together by energy which is constantly flowing. When one energy is weak, the others are weak as well. When one is stronger, it helps the others become stronger. The four levels include self, family, community, and the world.

Love yourself first. The more you love yourself, the more you can love others. It's difficult to give others what you can't give yourself first. It can be tough to love yourself sometimes. If you're like most men, you're harder on yourself than anyone else is.

That toughness can help you grow but it can also block out your healthy self-love. Take a moment to just love yourself. It will seem awkward at first, but after a while, you'll feel joy and contentment. The more love you have inside of you, the more you can give to others.

Next, love your family and friends as much as you can. These are the people closest to you, the ones that you can touch every day. Every so often, to reset the appreciation level, ask yourself what life would be like if you didn't have them around.

Love your community. The stronger your community is, the stronger your family will be as well. It may be easy to overlook your community because you're busy in your own world. But I can guarantee you, that there is at least one person in your community whose life you can impact today just by giving them a smile or some love.

And love your world. The Earth is an ecosystem that is impacted by every single living person. The energy you put out impacts billions of other people.

The air you breathe is the same oxygen that your neighbors breathe and the animals breathe. Think about this for a moment. The atoms that make up your body were likely part of another living being at some point in time. You have their energy in you and down the road, another living being will have your energy in them. There is only one planet Earth and it should be respected and loved.

Each of these four levels plays an important role in your life and your legacy.

Completing the Cycle

I truly believe that a man doesn't become complete until he has raised another man or at least mentored one. It's not until you have a son or another male under your wings that you realize what it takes to be a mindful alpha male. By teaching another male human being, you learn to be a Complete Man yourself.

There are a multitude of boys and men out there who need your help. They may not openly say it, but inside they are yearning it. Share what you have learned with others. Give them the chance to live the life they deserve to live, rather than the one they are stuck in. If this book has helped you in some way, share it with one other man you believe could benefit. There is no greater legacy than to guide others how to live a complete life.

The Time Is Now

You were meant to enjoy life. Your ultimate purpose is to be happy, and you deserve to have it all. You deserve to have a passionate relationship. You deserve freedom to do what you want, when you want.

How do you want to live your life? Or, to put it another way, what do you want people to say at your funeral? What do you want your wife to say about you? What do you want your kids to say about you? What do you want your friends to say about you?

Do you want them to say that you were an inComplete Man? Or do you want them to say that you lived life to the fullest, and that you had it all. That you had a life full of love, enjoyment, fulfillment, and happiness and you also showed others how to do the same.

I don't believe that legacy is about sacrifice or settling. It's not about the success you have or the money you make. It's not about the title you hold or the car you drive. I don't even believe it's about what you leave behind. I believe legacy is about living. Living the life you have ahead of you to the fullest. Legacy is life!

You've been given the tools to experience complete victory, to have it all. Now is your time to make it happen and enjoy it. Now is your time to be The Complete Man.

Summary Action Items

1. Don't wait until you…. Live your life now.

2. Focus on what's MOST important in your life.

3. Love as much as you can.

4. Focus on all four levels of impact: yourself, your family, your community and your world.

5. Mentor one man or boy on how to live a better life.

6. Legacy isn't what happens later, it's what happens now. Legacy is life.

7. Your time is NOW! Make it happen and enjoy it.

Congratulations! You've finished reading *The Complete Man*. Now it's time to start using the book's strategies and tactics in the book. Take that first step!

A good support system can be a big help in making that happen, and trying to do it alone is a major mistake. So please feel free to join our community of Complete Men. My team and I are here to support you and give you professional guidance, as we've done with so many other men.

You can personally text me (888) 210–5566 or email team@purdeepsangha.com. I will respond or someone on my team will respond promptly. Alternatively, you can call our office at 1 (866) 918-4140.

If you'd like further information, please visit:
www.PurdeepSangha.com

Now go and experience Complete Victory!

Sincerely,
Purdeep Sangha

ACKNOWLEDGEMENTS

A special thank you to my wife Ruby, my son Ranveer, and my daughter Dia for giving me the inspiration to write this book. Thanks also to my editor Mitch Sisskind and my research team: Michael Zweig, Aakarsh Sidharth, Vibha Bhat and Dr. Smriti Sharma.

ABOUT THE AUTHOR

Purdeep Sangha is the Founder and CEO of Sangha Worldwide, a global consulting and coaching firm providing group mastermind and one-on-one business and life coaching for corporate executives and entrepreneurs. Purdeep holds an Executive MBA in Innovation Leadership from the University of Fredericton and is a Certified Innovation Executive from a joint program of Stanford and MIT.

Purdeep is one of the few global experts who provide a holistic, comprehensive, and scientific approach to coaching men in business and human potential acceleration. He draws on neuroscience, performance psychology, and ancient teachings to help men get results beyond what they expect or even imagine. As a businessman himself, with a wife and two kids, Purdeep knows exactly what it takes to successfully balance career, family, and personal life. Most importantly, he knows how to communicate those principles in a way that gets results.

Through keynote speeches, in-person workshops, guest interviews, online training, and his podcast *The Male Entrepreneur*, Purdeep reaches a global audience of celebrity entrepreneurs, top executives in their field, and men from all walks of life who are determined to live completely. His mission is to create success and victory in the truest sense of those words.

www.PurdeepSangha.com